Dear Do

Hop

Love,

Michael

CW01646834

THE LIGHTS OF SINGAPORE

A LOVELY SINGAPORE EVENING

THE LIGHTS OF SINGAPORE

ROLAND BRADDELL

With 39 Illustrations

Kuala Lumpur
OXFORD UNIVERSITY PRESS
Oxford New York Melbourne
1982

Oxford University Press

Oxford London Glasgow
New York Toronto Melbourne Auckland
Kuala Lumpur Singapore Hong Kong Tokyo
Delhi Bombay Calcutta Madras Karachi
Nairobi Dar es Salaam Cape Town

and associates in
Beirut Berlin Ibadan Mexico City Nicosia

© T. L. Braddell 1966
First published by Methuen & Co. Ltd. 1934
First issued in Oxford in Asia Paperbacks *1982*

ISBN 0 19 582561 6

Cover illustration: View of the Victoria Memorial Hall, Singapore, 1934 (*Courtesy National Library, Singapore*)

Printed in Malaysia by Percetakan Mun Sun Sdn. Bhd., Shah Alam
Published by Oxford University Press, 3, Jalan 13/3,
Petaling Jaya, Selangor, Malaysia

CONTENTS

ILLUSTRATIONS

* *Photo: Nakajima, Singapore*
† „ *Theodore Hubback*
‡ „ *Ishii, Malacca*

NOTE TO THE READER

In this book—

MALAYA means that part of the Malay Peninsula which is either British or is under British protection; adjective, Malayan.

MALAYSIA means the Malay Peninsula and Malay Archipelago, often called Indonesia; adjective, Malaysian.

SOUTH-EASTERN ASIA means the territory included in Lower Burma, Siam, Indo-China, and Malaysia; often called Farther India.

THE LIGHTS OF SINGAPORE

IT had been one of our perfect Singapore evenings. The setting sun had left behind a whirl of pink opal where the clouds jostled each other against the west. To the east the sky was topaz, lemon, and turquoise, while the sea took on a myriad impossible tints and the trees and slopes opposite to the rock on which we stood showed rifle-green. A kingfisher flashed by, his wings like the dream of a rainbow ; and up overhead a great eagle hovered golden brown.

The beauty of it kept us rooted until here and there lights jerked out of the dusk and flares blazed up on distant fishing-stakes. A mosque drum began to throb—*pong ticka-tick tick*, *pong ticka-tick tick*—and soon there followed the sing-song drone of Mohammedan prayer.

Then all unawares the sudden night shut down and the stars began to sing.

The drive back from the inland coast after dinner was cool and sweet. A refreshing breeze had sprung up and blew a steady stream through our house at Tanjong Katong, which means Turtle Point. As I leaned out from an upstair window and looked across the Roads, the lights of Singapore were whispering tales to a sickle moon. So I lifted my wine cup, as the Chinese poet has sung, and questioned the blue night-sky; and romance was the answer it sent.

To find the wonder that lies in the lights of most cities, you must look into them from outside, but to see the lights of Singapore as they should be seen you must watch them riding against the deep sapphire curtain of the night in the Roads, whence the waterways beckon you out to the Spice Islands and the enchanted seas.

There ride the lights of great cargo steamers and of men-o'-war, but far more interesting are the lights which twinkle from a host of comfortable little steamers that fuss up and down to Java and Sumatra, to the Spice Islands, to Indo-China, to Borneo, Sarawak, and Siam, or round the east and west coasts of the Malay Peninsula. Alongside them but more to the east lie hundreds of fat Chinese junks and slim Malay schooners, folded in their night's sleep. What wonderful yarns they could spin of typhoon and monsoon, of sun-kissed seas, of spices and drugs, of quaint quays and lovely islands, of violent sudden deaths and violent sudden loves. As one looks at them they turn in one's imagination into the high-pooped ships of lusty Portuguese, Dutch, and British adventurers; or, turning back still further the leaves of history, one sees phantoms gliding through the night that tell of all the early adventurers, Indians, Greeks, Chinese, Arabs, Persians and before them, some say, even Egyptians and Phoenicians.

Our past, like our future, lies upon the seas that surround us, and I shall tell you later something of that past, so that when, as tourists will, you go through the wonderlands which you can reach from Singapore, you may realize the better the romance of what you are seeking and may know what brave feet have trod before you, what strong keels have ploughed the seas your ship will pass.

When you come into Singapore the whole place seems so new, so very George the Fifth. Up overhead seaplanes circle; opposite the wharves is a brand-new railway station; you roll into town along a road both sides of which implore you not to be vague but to order Haig, or to try somebody's silk stockings or somebody else's cigarettes; the streets are full of motor traffic; most of the big buildings which you pass seem quite new; and, if you are English, you get an impression of a kind of tropical cross between Manchester and Liverpool. The only ruins you will see are either clutching a whisky and soda or proferring a beggar's bowl. You inquire and are told that Singapore was founded in 1819 by Sir Stamford Raffles—whoever he may be, you probably think to yourself.

So the place seems to have no ancient history, no romantic background. As an English lady resident once said to me: 'I don't see how you can find any interest in this place beyond the obvious. It has no history like India or China'; and that is the general impression. But history is written on the seas as well as on the land, and the romance of trade is as great as that of the cities and buildings created by that trade. Every month there pass by my house at Tanjong Katong the mercantile flags of all the major nations of the world, beside all manner of quaint native craft; and I seem to see the world's trade passing backward and forward in front of my garden, and to watch shapes and sails to find the origin of which you must penetrate to the very dawn of history. If there is any more romantic tale in the history of the world than that of the Spice Trade I do not know it, nor do I know anything which has played a greater part in that history. It built up the power of Solomon, of Tyre and Sidon, of Rome, of Venice, of Alexandria, of Bagdad; it sent Christopher Columbus to America, Vasco da Gama round one Cape and Magellan round the other; it fed with its riches Portugal, Holland, and Great Britain; and from it grew the British Empire in India. It upset more than once the economics of the West and the Far East, disturbed the balance of gold, and played its part in human morals and human behaviour through the

THE INNER ROADS, SINGAPORE

THE LIVING ROOM

THE DINING ROOM

MY HOUSE IN "UNCULTURED" SINGAPORE

luxuries which it scattered so lavishly. And the heart and marrow of that trade lay in Malaysia, and over Malaysian waters it was carried, most of it past the very spot where I watch the ships to-day.

If, then, you are interested in world history, or are searching for romantic lands and seas, let the lights of Singapore lead you. You will find, indeed, that, though the town itself contains much of interest, it is as a pushing-off place that Singapore makes its greatest claim to your attention, if you are a tourist. From it you can get comfortably and safely to more interesting places, I do believe, than from anywhere else in the world, and, when your appetite is satisfied, the great liners will carry you where you will—a Clapham Junction of the world, served, so they tell me, by some eighty lines of steamers!

So the lights twinkle and beckon to the seas and the romantic lands around us, but in the town they flare over many curious things and quaint sights.

Wherever I have been throughout the world, I have always found the greatest interest in Singapore (particularly in the United States), for there seems to be something in the name that stirs the imagination; but I have also found the most amazing ignorance and the most absurd notions. If one wants to find out about the place, there are, of course, plenty of books of various kinds, but as yet there is none which will give you history without tears, and such facts as you are liable to want to know in easily digestible doses. This book tries to supply that want; and if at times it travels outside Singapore, that is necessary and, I hope, helpful to a better understanding of what the place means and has meant in the past.

In reading this book will you please imagine that you and I are chatting together after dinner and I am holding forth, as hosts will, about the things that interest me in the hope that they will interest you?

THE CAMPHOR-WOOD BOX

I DO not know exactly what is the fascination of life in Singapore for so many of us, nor do I believe that any book could convey it, but I do know that, sons and grandsons, nephews and grand-nephews, we have a most disconcerting way of coming back—disconcerting, that is to say, to our parents who almost invariably vow during our extreme infancy that no child of theirs shall ever live in the tropics.

One simply has got to be born where one's mother happens to be at the time, and that fact explains why I was born in Singapore and my father in Province Wellesley, which is on the mainland of the Peninsula opposite Penang. We were each of us dispatched to England during the first four years of our lives, were educated there at school and at Oxford, were duly called to the Bar (he at the Inner and I at the Middle Temple) and then to the annoyance of our respective parents scampered back to Singapore. Our fathers had destined each of us for the Woolsack, but the sojourn of many generations of ancestors in Counties Wicklow and Wexford, Ireland, had made us too easy-going or too sensible to try even for a solitary brief in the Temple, much less for the prize of prizes.

Many people, and Americans in particular, find it surprising that the English should be content to live in their tropical colonies and to be separated from their children, and even more surprising that those children should return and go through the same process themselves. I do not know, as I said before, what is the true explanation, but I will tell you a story about a small boy whom I knew very well and who grew to be a man, whom, alas! I am beginning to find that I know only too well.

It is 1887, the year of Queen Victoria's Jubilee, and the place is a tall house in Kensington. Outside there is the thickest of fogs, a real London particular. In the distance and coming slowly nearer, for he makes many stops, is that cheeriest of sounds, the bell of the muffin-man. The small boy is curled up in front of a bright fire, with a huge black cat in his arms. Earlier that year he had come from his mother's father in Dover to stay with his father's parents in London, but he is very happy. London is so much more exciting than Dover, though he misses very badly his other grandfather and the yacht and the soldiers and the wonderful reviews and his beautiful aunts.

Here in London marvellous things are always

happening. On Tuesdays, Punch and Judy comes, and his grandmother has a cup of tea for the proprietor and a bone for dog Toby, and one hears some interesting things if one sits quite still and says nothing. On Fridays, the old Scotsman plays his bagpipes up the street, while his pretty daughter dances the Highland Fling. The very tradesmen give one the most tremendous thrills. There's the reckless butcher's boy, with his pomaded bare head and his blue-and-white apron, who races round the corner every morning on one wheel of his high dog-cart, and from whom one can sometimes sneak a ride when Grannie is out. There's the milk-man, with his cheery cry of 'Milk-oh,' a man who can produce ha'pennies out of one's nose or ears, a man of talents. The boy to this day never smells slightly sour milk without hearing a ghostly 'Milk-oh,' or expecting a ghostly ha'penny to come from his head. Then, most astonishing of all, the knife-grinder; very terrifying, though, for he is a wild gipsy-looking fellow, with a bloodthirsty collection of cutlery round his barrow. Yet he will sometimes let one turn the grindstone while he sharpens, and one always listens eagerly for his wailing 'Scissors and Knives to Grind-oh.' He has the most ghastly collection of stories about London murders that he tells in a husky voice, with a ghoul-like relish, and that send one up the long flight of stairs to bed in a sweat of fright. Then there is the glittering Café Royal, where one is sometimes taken to join grandfather after his tiffin, as he persists in calling his midday meal. Orpen's picture, which sometimes hangs in the Jeu de Paume in Paris, ought to contain a very goggle-eyed little boy who neglects his ice-cream to stare at a funny little man with a curious voice called Mr. Whistler, and a most extraordinarily dressed fattish man called Mr. Wilde, or a bearded laughing man apparently called Georgear Sims, a truly strange Christian name that makes him a source of much wonder. Then there were the Nigger Minstrels, and the bus-drivers, with their gorgeous lies about Tel-el-Kebir and Kandahar and other places where their personal valour saved the day for England. And heaps of other things that you could not write about the London of to-day.

But it is the servants' hall down in the basement of his grandfather's house that holds the happiest memories for our small boy. Here is an old Welsh housekeeper-cook with an endless chain of uncanny folk-tales. Her daughter is his grandmother's maid and her son his grandfather's valet. She has another perfectly terrific son who is a sergeant in the Metropolitan Police and, when that son pays his weekly visit, the small boy squirms with joy. Ever since in his heart has dwelt an abiding affection for the London Bobbie. There is also a small page-boy, full of original sin and bubbling with mischief; he didn't last long, though; he had too many ideas. Our small boy, it need hardly be said, spends most of his time in the servants' hall and in the kitchen.

This afternoon, however, he is in his grandmother's sitting-room, all alone in front of the fire, with the thick fog outside, and, as he gazes into the flames, his mind wanders through his little life, for he is not yet seven years old. He cannot remember his mother or his father, since he was separated from them when he was barely three and a half, but dimly through the flames he sees a brake of sugar-cane and some pommeloe trees—very strange—and he cannot remember where he saw them nor at the time did he even know what they were. He sees quaint shadow-shapes on a white screen, and other children are seated beside him, and he knows that they are all in the saloon of a ship, but he can't remember why. And then he sees, most wondrous of all, an old Chinese staggering up a red drive-way with a gigantic rocking-horse. Ah, he remembers that perfectly! Didn't he take the eyes out of that horse every evening so that it could not see to run away during the night? Now, where could that rocking-horse be? He must ask his Grannie when she comes back from the concert. What on earth *was* a concert anyway? Must be something nice or people would not drive off to see it.

Then Fred the valet breaks in upon him and says, 'I am going to get out your grandfather's uniform. Would you like to come?' He would, indeed. There was a thing called a Reception and a person called the Prince, and in some strange way they were connected with his grandfather's blue-and-gold uniform and the red leather case containing the C.M.G. and the Perak war medal.

Up in grandfather's room there was a carved box made from the wood of a real Malayan camphor tree, and he had often wanted to see what was inside it. So, while Fred is busy with the uniform case, our small boy lifts the lid of the wooden box, and, as he does so, there comes out of it a strange arresting smell that makes the little boy's senses reel. It is not the camphor smell alone, for he knows that quite well. There is something mixed with it; a strange smell of mould and damp hot earth sweating after rain, that unforgettable smell which arises when any box is opened that has lain long in the tropics. The small boy knows that smell; it is connected with the cane-brake and the Chinese and the rocking-horse. Somehow it means that mythical father and mother of his who are in some strange place at the other end of the world called

Singapore. It brings a great lump into his throat, and tears stream down his face. He wants to race out of the house and run to Singapore and find his mother again, and feel long-forgotten arms round his small thin body once more.

Never again will he be able to forget that fog-laden afternoon or that strange pulling smell. All his life's recollections will start from that moment and wander from it backwards or forwards. It is as vivid to-day as it was all those long years ago. It comes to him as he lies awake in England or France or America, or wherever he may be during his long leaves; and always it tugs him back as it did then. It is the scent of the East; the scent that has lured men since the dawn of history to the seas of Malaya, and that will continue to lure them until the curtain drops on history.

BELIEVE IT OR NOT

'SO you come from Singapore—but how intriguing! Then you can tell me all about the monsoons. You know, those funny little things that run about in the punkahs and kill snakes! '

Well, that's about as accurate as most outside information about Singapore; and it will serve to introduce you to our 'terrible climate.' In Singapore the weather is like that of every other place—most unusual for the time of the year; and we generally blame it on the monsoons. 'It's between monsoons' or 'The monsoon hasn't broken yet' or 'The monsoon is very late this year'; you'll hear plenty about it in these parts. It is important for you to know about these winds, for they affect one's comfort very materially.

The word is derived from the Arabic *mausim*, meaning season, and a monsoon is a seasonal wind caused by the summer heating of the land masses of Asia and then by their winter cooling. There are accordingly two monsoons: the south-west or summer one, blowing from May to October, and the north-east or winter one, blowing from November to April. At the end of each there is a very wet period of about one month when the winds are light and variable. Singapore is so near the Equator that the monsoons have quite a different effect from what they have in India. The south-west is hardly felt at all; the north-east, though much stronger, in nothing like the ferocity which it displays in the Gulf of Siam or the South China Sea; but both are very welcome visitors. The north-east is the cooler one, bringing plenty of rain and lots of cold nights; it is then that the big round-the-world tourist ships come, and the ordinary liners give forth their full quotas of visitors. Singapore always wakes up in the north-east monsoon, and the hotel people and the shopkeepers grin round the town like the dogs of the Psalmist.

The south-west monsoon is drier and warmer and is the season for sports, when a garden-party can be planned in safety and when the full moons can be relied upon to make a fairyland for the romantic. And talking of moons you would never believe some of ours. In September and October the full moon comes up exactly like the setting sun, a great crimson ball; it slowly changes into a deep orange, then gradually passes through the orange tints into the yellows. It comes up smack in the middle of a bright blue sky, and not until it stands right overhead and night has long since fallen does it turn white. The first time I saw it I was playing golf on the old racecourse and I could not make up my mind whether I had gone mad or the sun had missed the way out. Once going into Penang harbour a kindly captain called me just at dawn and showed me the risen sun astern and the full moon sinking ahead with the sky in between, such an opal as no one could paint or describe. I hope that you may have as good luck some day.

What is the best season to travel to or from Europe through the Suez Canal ? I have often been asked that question, and much practice has taught me that travelling in either direction you should start at the end of February and arrive in March. You will find the Indian Ocean quite cool and just a playful pond, while the Red Sea is cold. But if you are going home after a long period here, I recommend you to tarry awhile in the north of Italy or the south of France and not to go north till spring has fully burgeoned, as the poets say.

In Singapore we get no typhoons or cyclones and no earthquakes ; our only abnormal unpleasantnesses are violent squalls of wind and rain. These come only during the south-west monsoon, and we call them 'Sumatras,' because they are caused by the monsoon being obstructed in its course by the mountains of Sumatra. The wind during these squalls, which frequently cover a front of as much as three hundred miles, usually comes from a south-west or westerly direction and is invariably accompanied by blinding rain, making navigation in the Straits of Malacca extremely hazardous. Ashore the wind and rain blow with fury against the houses, so that, if one's windows and doors are not shut tight, Aunt Mary's photograph is blown from one room to another, the curtains stand out at right angles, and falling objects beat a tattoo everywhere. The whole thing, however, passes as quickly as it comes, and the 'Sumatras' are well understood, giving plenty of warning to the wise that they are on their way.

Our 'terrible climate' is in reality quite a reasonable one, though enervating. May and June are the most disagreeable months, owing to the prevalence of the southerly winds which we call 'Java winds.' It is remarkable that the stronger these winds blow the more enervating they are, and this is particularly noticeable at Katong on the seacoast. They also generally bring colds and minor fevers, particularly influenza and dengue, so that the Malays call them expressively *angin jehat*, or evil winds.

It is seldom, at any time of the year, that the mornings and nights are not cool, since diurnal breezes from land or sea blow over the island. The afternoons between half-past two and four o'clock are usually very hot. Mean temperature in the shade through the year is about 81°·5 F. The highest to which the shade thermometer is liable to go is 90° F. and the lowest 73°·5 F. Generally speaking you can say that the shade temperature will range most of the time between 76° F. and 87° F. The heat, then, is not great, but it is continuous and, of course, humid, so that the newcomer feels it very much. Moreover, many people only know Singapore from shipboard or hotel; they accordingly regard it as much hotter and more uncomfortable than it really is, so that exaggerated notions get spread.

Nowadays the sun is regarded as a friend and not an enemy, as it was when I first came out. You will see people at the seaside sunbathing as though they were in the South of France, and doctors are recommending people not to fear the sun. The newcomer, however, would be wise to be careful until properly acclimatized.

It is curious that Singapore, which in its early days was a health station for officers of the East India Company, should have acquired a reputation for bad health. The general death-rate in 1932 was 20·12 per mille, and last year (1933) it has sometimes fallen to between 18 and 19.[1] Consider that as against a death-rate for a city of similar size in Europe or America, which would

[1] After I wrote the above, the death-rate fell to 16·66 per mille for the week ending October 7, 1933.

be from 11 to 15 per mille, and bear in mind the overcrowding in the purely Asiatic parts of the town, the ignorance of hygiene amongst the lowest classes and the fact that numbers of Asiatics from up-country come here to the sick houses of their own nationalities, and die here from causes with which Singapore has nothing whatsoever to do. The fact is that so far from being unhealthy, Singapore is really the opposite, and it is interesting to see why this is so.

In the first place, we have a magnificent water supply, which, carried in pipes for some forty miles from a mountain in Johore, is so pure that the Municipal Health Officer recommends people to drink it unfiltered from the taps. This water is chlorinated. An interesting fact about such water seems to have emerged. Dr. Heiser, the well-known expert of the Rockefeller Institute, has observed that wherever a town has adopted chlorination of its water supply, no matter how bacteriologically pure that supply had been in the first instance, there has been practically an immediate improvement in the general death-rate.

Week after week the League of Nations Health Bureau in its tabulations of the cities of the Orient marks *nil* against Singapore in respect of smallpox, plague, and cholera. When people are dying like flies in China or India or elsewhere,

Singapore remains strangely immune, and the reasons apparently are these. Our rats very obligingly only carry an average of three plague fleas each; our vaccination is widespread and effective; and our water supply and Health Department highly efficient. I suspect also that our climate has a lot to do with it. As for the rest of the pests of the Orient, spinal fever, diphtheria, dysentery, and typhoid are very rare, the last being due almost entirely to the itinerant food-hawkers. Tuberculosis, malaria, and the venereal diseases with their sequelæ would seem to account for the bulk of the general death-rate.

Turning to the white peoples, it can be said with absolute truth that given a normally healthy constitution a white man or woman can keep as well in Singapore as anywhere else, provided that he or she leads a healthy, normal life and takes the necessary amount of long leave. Alcohol is man's worst enemy here, and most emphatically woman's; not that you will see drunken people about, for you won't. I don't mean that at all. Neurasthenia hovers around out here; people feel let down, they apply alcohol and a vicious circle results. It is the frequency of the applications, not their potency, to which I refer. The real fact is that the climate gets blamed for all sorts of things which really boil down to over-exercise, over-eating, or over-drinking; and they are liable to happen anywhere.

The actual death-rate for Europeans (which expression includes all white people from wheresoever they come) was 6·92 per mille in 1932 and 6·53 in 1931. So don't be the least bit afraid to come to Singapore.

And what about life here? I received from my father advice which he received from his, the accumulated wisdom of Singapore ancients, as it were; and I am only too glad to pass it on.

'If you want to be healthy, never take an entirely cold bath, never sleep at night with your stomach uncovered, put disinfectant immediately on any kind of a cut or skin abrasion, and use alcohol just as a sane-living person would in Europe.

'If you want to be happy, remember that the country is just round the corner waiting to black-jack you. Don't admit that you are living in an Oriental country; live as nearly as possible as you would in Europe. Read plenty, the mind needs more exercise than the body; keep yourself up to date; have your own things round you, and as much beauty as you can in your home. Above all, never wear a sarong and baju; that's the beginning of the end!'

The fact is, that every white man who goes to the Orient has a mental and spiritual fight before him; he must always keep up his guard or the country will down him. It has been said that Singapore is a paradise for second-class people, and so it is in one way; but, however second-class their talents may be, only first-class people can remain captains of their souls, and that goes double for the Orient.

So far as creature comforts are concerned, Singapore will do you proud—all kinds of sport all the year round, a good table, owing to cold storage, and a magnificent fish supply, comfortable houses, lovely green gardens, superb roads on which to motor, and plenty of places to go by road, rail, or sea. Perhaps the best thing about our life is that we are forced to take longish periods of leave, so that we get better chances of seeing the world than our opposite numbers at home, most of whom take a fortnight or a month each year for their annual holiday and go nowhere much when they take it.

The newcomer will find that he has to work very hard in Singapore; there is no such *dolce far niente* as people are wont to connect with a tropical life, no shutting down for a couple or more hours at midday as there is in the Dutch Indies or Indo-China. Except for public holidays, work goes on all the year round and, though employers are beginning to realize the value of short periods of local leave, it has not yet become a habit of business life here. The sooner it does, the better, because local leave is a fine tonic, and the mental change involved more than pays the employer for the temporary loss of the employee's service.

Singapore has an extraordinary reputation for wild night-life and opium dens and so forth, so I find when I am *in partibus*. I see that Mr. Hendrik van Loon in his recent best-seller on geography, after remarking that Singapore 'will play a great part when the inevitable clash between the East and West finally takes place,' goes on: 'In anticipation of that event, it maintains a set of bar-rooms, the splendour of which is famous all over the Orient, and loses almost as much money on the annual races as the city of Dublin.' And that is the kind of thing that is disseminated continually throughout the world; but not, mark you, by any one who really knows Singapore or has even been here for more than a couple of weeks.

Will Rogers came here under the usual impression, and wrote back to America that the wickedest thing he found here was the Dutch wife (a long bolster) that was in his bed.

Mark Hellinger, New York columnist, said this is an interview:

'You know, I was one of those fellows who thought Singapore was just the lousiest place; one of the cesspools of the world. You've probably got the same mistaken idea of Hollywood.'

'The films taught me about tigers, drunken boobs, and fallen dames struggling to get back to the borders of civilization—and, why, I can't get a "one o'clock" after 12 midnight!

'And Singapore, I find, is the cleanest city I've struck anywhere. In what sense? Why, every sense. It's clean and nice—and is it sober?

'I'm going to write four or five articles about Singapore, and the first will tell Broadway just what a big mistake she's made.'

And Fleet Street is as bad as Broadway. Only the other day I read how the fishermen in Singapore often pull up tigers in their nets!

I am continually reading in our newspapers here that there is no culture in Singapore, and I often wonder what precisely the writers mean. I am inclined to believe that wherever you find a cultured man or woman you have culture; it is up to the individual. We have a concert hall and world-famous musicians frequently play here, but only a handful ever goes to hear them. We have a splendid library at the back of Raffles Museum, but outside of the section containing novels how many use it? We have started an art collection with some of Dora Gordine's finest work, counterparts of which are or will be in the Tate Gallery, but how many people will truly appreciate them? If there is no culture in Singapore, it is because the majority of the white people spend their leisure time doing things with various kinds of balls as Anglo-Saxons do all over the world. Personally, I have never found it at all difficult to keep abreast with what is going on all over the world in the realms of 'culture'—a horrible word when used in that sense.

If by culture they mean civilization, then I suggest that Malaya is a gold mine for the cultural anthropologist, and affords a great chance to any young professional who could afford to spend two years here. He will find an almost virgin field, save for such work as linguists and students of the Malayan Civil Service have done in purely Malay matters.

What, then, are the drawbacks in this garden of Eden, you will sarcastically ask me? Plenty!

Exhibit A is the Hailam servant, a most exasperating person. He has only one way of doing things, his own; he only cleans what he sees; he is very communistic, very stupid, and, as a cook, can be guaranteed to take all the taste out of anything, unless carefully supervised and trained. There are, doubtless, brilliant exceptions, but through and by I have never found worse servants than the present-day Hailams.

Exhibit B is a general and totally nerve-racking inefficiency. Nothing seems to be 100 per cent.; nothing ever seems to be done right the first time. The result is such a wear and tear on the nervous system as only the entirely callous can combat.

Exhibits A and B, in my belief, explain most of the so-called tropical neurasthenia with which white people are troubled.

Exhibit C is a more than ordinarily British conservatism which amounts almost to a condition of mental sclerosis, as it were. The exponent of any idea that, however well known elsewhere, is new to Singapore has first to get across three fences; and they are marked respectively, 'It can't be done,' 'It has never been done before,' and 'Now is not the time to do it.' This accounts for so much in Singapore that is noticeably behind the times in the midst of so much that is right abreast of them, and it undoubtedly leads to a great deal of irritation, as you will find in particular when you go shopping or house-furnishing or decorating.

And there are many other things that are drawbacks; noises, smells, insects, and such like, that you will find in any Oriental city. Worst of all is the parting of children from their parents. Believe it or not, Malaya possesses no real hill station as yet, unless Fraser's Hill merits such a description; millions and millions of dollars have for years been spent annually on this, that, and the other, but no one so far has given the country an obvious necessity, though a very protracted beginning is at last being made at Cameron Highlands in Pahang. Even Penang Hill, which we have possessed since A.D. 1786, is for all practical purposes undeveloped.

There is one last point that I would make for those who contemplate coming here to live. It has been so admirably said by a Dutch lady, Madelon Lulofs, in her recent novel, *Rubber* (which you certainly must read), that, if she will permit me, I will quote:

'What he did not realize—what no one who leaves his own country realizes—is that never again would he be at home anywhere. Not in this new land, where he had spent his best years, and not in the old land, where his youth had been, where perhaps his old age was to be. He did not realize that nowhere would he find a corner all his own, and that never again would he belong to a country, to a people. For behind him a door had slammed irrevocably. Life holds no door open for any man.'

That, of course, is a matter of the spirit; you will still remain an Englishman or an American or whatever you are, but work out here for twenty years or more and you will know the truth of what I have quoted. It is for me both the tragedy and the comedy of a life such as I have led that you see the world with equal eyes, and not as national and racial prejudices pretend that it is. You find that you are as much at home in Batavia or Honolulu or Tokio or Shanghai or Paris or Berlin or Rome as you are in London or New York—perhaps more so. The old prejudices, the old inhibitions, the old superiorities, the old snobberies have dropped off you like the slough from a snake, and you wake up to find yourself a citizen of everywhere but a citizen of nowhere—unless, of course, you are one of those happily parochial people whom nothing can wean from the one small spot from which they come. If you are of these last, I am not sure but that you are not among the truly chosen people, those elected to carry on the job of *homo sapiens*, the anchors of our civilization.

DRAGON-TEETH GATE

YOUR liner will duly come into Singapore Harbour, the approach to which is believed to be one of the most beautiful in the world. It will then berth alongside the Singapore Harbour Board wharves, and you will thus find yourself in one of the world's famous narrows, the real Old Strait of Singapore, the western mouth of which was called Dragon-Teeth Gate by the ancient Chinese mariners.

The fact that here was the Old Strait came to be forgotten when the passage fell into disuse after European sailors came into our waters. Their ships had no sweeps like the Asiatic craft, and the fierce currents were too much for them; so they turned aside into the present main strait of Singapore, which they called Governor's Strait. The map of Godinho de Eredia, dated A.D. 1604, shows that the present Keppel Harbour was the Old Strait, but for many years it was thought (and the mistake is still being repeated continually) that the present Straits of Johore formed the passage that the ancient mariners used. These last straits, however, could never have been used owing to the unnecessarily laborious business of sailing through them and, still more so, owing to the danger of pirates with whom all the waters round Singapore abounded, and against whom the ancient records contain many warnings.

At the western entrance to Keppel Harbour there used long ago to be two pointed rocks, one on the end of the island of Blakang Mati, and one where the present white stone marking the harbour limit stands, called Lot's Wife; but these rocks from their nearness to each other proved an obstruction to navigation, so they were blown up about eighty-five years ago, after Captain (the late Admiral of the Fleet, Sir) Harry Keppel had rediscovered the Strait, which is now called Keppel Harbour after him, though at first and for long termed New Harbour. These two rocks reminded the Chinese of the two upright pegs in the bows of their junks through which the cable runs; and, as these pegs are called 'dragon's teeth,' they gave the name Dragon-Teeth Gate to the entrance to the Strait. Old descriptions all refer to the narrowness of the entrance, one written in A.D. 1599 saying that 'from the ship you could jump ashore or touch the branches of the trees on either side.'

There are two ancient Chinese books, one written in A.D. 1350 and called *Description of the Barbarians of the Isles*, and the other written

GODINHO DA EREDIA'S MAP, 1604

ESTREITO VELHO = OLD STRAIT; ESTREITO NOVO = NEW STRAIT;
XABANDARIA = HARBOUR-MASTER'S OFFICE

in A.D. 1436 and bearing the truly delightful name *Description of the Starry Raft*, which contain descriptions of the Old Strait. I quote from the former :

'The Strait is bordered by two hills of the Tan-ma-hsi (Singapore) barbarians which look like dragon's teeth ; between them is a waterway. The soil is poor and ricefields few. The climate is hot and in the fourth and fifth moons there are very heavy rains. The people are addicted to piracy.'

There follows a reference to the customs of the people and to their Chief ; and then the description proceeds :

'When Chinese junks go to the western sea these people let them pass unmolested, but when on the way back they have reached Carimon Island then the junk people get out their armour and padded screens against arrow fire to protect themselves, for of a certainty two or three hundred pirate junks will come out to attack them. Sometimes they may have good luck and a favouring wind and they may not catch up with them ; if not, then the crews are all butchered and the merchandise made off with in short order.'

Doubtless this last is an exaggerated picture of the dangers from piracy, or trade could not have thrived ; but for centuries Singapore had a reputation for piracy, and Munshi Abdullah, the Malay clerk of Raffles, describing the island as it was when the British came in 1819, wrote:

'At that time no mortal dared to pass through the Straits of Singapore. Jinns and Satans even were afraid, for that was the place the pirates made use of, to sleep at and divide their booty, after a successful attack on any ship's boats or *prahus*. There also they put to death their captives, and themselves fought and killed each other in their quarrels over the division of the spoil.

'All along the beach there were hundreds of human skulls, some of them old, some fresh with the hair still remaining, some with the teeth still sharp, and some without teeth.'

The Malays in those days regarded trade as beneath contempt, but piracy as quite the thing; and this appears from a conversation that has been recorded between Raffles and the Temenggong of Singapore. It took the British very many years and plenty of fighting before they stamped out Malay piracy.

So when your ship ties up remember that, although the poor dragon long since lost his teeth, you are in his maw and you would never believe what that maw and its surroundings looked like when I tied up on September 1, 1905.

Tanjong Pagar wharves at that time were

made of wood, standing on great wooden piles, into which the teredo worms were continually eating their way. Back of them was all swamp, with a narrow carriage-road swinging through it and taking one into town. But a twentieth-century Aladdin summoned his Jinns and said, 'Let this swamp become one of the world's greatest ports'; and the name of that Aladdin was Sir John Rumney Nicholson, and his Jinns were the great English contractors, John Aird & Company, and Topham, Jones, & Railton.

So I watched Mount Erskine and Mount Palmer and many other small hills being hacked and hewed and spewed into the swamps, great areas of reclamation created, the tide beaten back foot by foot to its present race, great walls of granite rising forty feet from the concreted bed of dried-out swamp, the sea brooked and curbed and shut out by more granite walls, until to-day all trace of the great swamp has gone and it is impossible to guess its boundaries. Back of the wharves and on the other side of the wide road that swings into town where the old carriage-road used to run, you will see a railway with sheds and sidings and huge blocks of quarters and a fine big station, all standing where the old swamp sent up its fetid smells at low tide. I rub my eyes still with astonishment at what I saw done in those six years between 1908 and 1914.

Those who are accustomed to docks in Europe and America with their usually evil surroundings will be struck by the picture which ours present —not a slum, not an offensive sight, they form with the railway at the back a picture unequalled in the town, and so far as I know unequalled in any other of the world's great ports.

From your ship lying in the Dragon's maw you will see the chimneys of the Straits Trading Company's works at Pulau Brani, where a very large proportion of the world's tin is smelted. You will also notice a Malay village built over the water, from which the diving boys come to amuse you. The inhabitants of this village are believed to be the descendants of the original *Orang Laut* (Sea Men) whom Raffles found in Singapore in 1819.

If you run out east to spend the cool of an evening at the Sea View Hotel in Tanjong Katong you will travel over another fine wide road (the Grove Road) which did not exist when I first came, and you will see the little trains chugging back and forth as work proceeds on another great piece of reclamation. Here another port is being made, but this time an air-port; and the Aladdin who has rubbed the lamp on this occasion is our present Governor, Sir Cecil Clementi, who alone saw the possibility of the site (which he did very appropriately from an aeroplane) and in face of much opposition carried his way; and his Jinns come from the Public Works Department under Mr. Sturrock and Mr. St. George Caulfield.

On completion this new air-port will provide accommodation for both land and seaplanes, and will be one of the largest and best equipped in the East. Its site is quite unique, since it is within two miles from the heart of the town, and its importance will be great, both from an imperial and an international point of view, since it lies on the main route between England and Australia, and between Java and Holland, while it will also be the centre of subsidiary air lines branching out to all parts of the Malay Archipelago, in addition to being the terminus of the eastern and western Malayan air routes that are to be created.

The site now being filled in is a pestilential swamp with squalid surroundings, but, when the work is completed, the scene should be attractive, with a grass-covered circular air-field, one thousand yards in diameter, and neat buildings and hangars around it. The total area to be reclaimed amounts to 339 acres, and work is proceeding at the rate of 200,000 tons a month, the earth being cut out from hills four miles away. The cost is estimated at over six million Straits dollars, and will be met entirely out of accumulated reserves.

We are very air-minded in Singapore to-day,

and are proud that ours was the first city in the Empire to start a private seaplane flying club. Weekly Dutch services run to Java and to Holland, and soon a British service between England and Australia is to begin. At present the landplanes use the Royal Air Force field at Seletar, and the seaplanes the small sheltered bay opposite the Yacht Club.

But whatever the future may hold for us in the air, to-day we live by the seas. Into and from this great port there entered and cleared in 1932, 44,407 vessels of 30,415,107 tons burthen, despite the fact that in that year 20 per cent. of the world's shipping was laid up. Our peak year was 1930, with nearly thirty-four million tons; and when trade resumes its full functioning our docks will not be big enough, so that large extensions are now being planned.

Compare those figures with 1833, when a total of 2074 ships, with a tonnage of 172,225, visited Singapore, which then contained a population of 20,978 as against its half-million to-day.

Stamford Raffles stands in front of the Victoria Memorial gazing from his pedestal at the spot where tradition has always said that he first landed, and, if his spirit ever returns here, as one hopes it does, what must be his pride! If ever a man was entitled to say 'I told you so,' that man is our great founder.

I have referred much to reclamation, and there

COLLYER QUAY, SINGAPORE
THE WHOLE FRONT OF WHICH HAS BEEN RECLAIMED FROM THE SEA

VIEW FROM THE ESPLANADE, SINGAPORE, 1840
THE ROAD RUNS ABOUT WHERE THE CRICKET PITCHES ARE TO-DAY

OVER THE ROOFS OF CHINATOWN, SINGAPORE

is a curious difference which you will note between the British and the Dutch in their enterprises in this part of the world. The latter build up rivers, while we push out into the sea.

Ever since Singapore was founded man has been wrestling with the sea and the swamps. Raffles Square, the business heart of the town, was originally a swamp filled in by cutting down a hill at the point of the river. So we proceeded; the low hills were cut down until the town seemed big enough, but it grew and more hills were lowered and more swamps filled. Still it grew, but we would not be pressed inland; more hills were cut down and tilted into the sea, and the tide was pushed back so that practically the whole front of our town is reclamation. The Padang, as we call the big playing-field opposite the Municipal Offices, was originally half its present depth, and the entire drive from the Docks to Raffles Hotel is almost all the way over land reclaimed from the sea or swamp, much of it quite recently; and even to-day, as I write, we are still at it with more reclamation proceeding opposite Raffles Hotel and the Drill Hall.

It has been intensely interesting to me during the past twenty-eight years to watch Singapore growing, and more interesting still to have taken a very little part in the planning of that growth. It is good to peer into the future and try to out-guess Fate, good to plan for health and recreation, good to see playgrounds arise out of slums, good to see children playing where brothels used to be, and good to watch the death-rate fall and the birth-rate rise year by year. The citizens of Singapore run their own town, and there are no more useful public jobs here than those of the Municipal Commissioners and the Improvement Trustees. They hold the future in their hands.

Government moves slowly its wonders to perform, but when it does, it performs for permanence and builds successfully. I remember once taking two Americans round the town and showing them our big public works and buildings. They asked me how they were 'bonded,' as Americans call it, and when I replied that for the greater part they were done out of accumulated revenues, they would not believe me at first, but finally one of them observed, 'Well, going round the world has shown me what a lot we have to learn from you Britishers, and financing public works is one of the things.'

It is irritating not to get all the improvements one wants immediately one wants them, but by waiting until we have the money to pay for them we escape debt, and so have much cause for gratitude to the wise financiers of the past and the present. By this careful finance the Colony, and Singapore in particular, has stood up splendidly to the economic storms of the past four years; we have large surpluses, little public debt, low taxation, and a more than balanced budget. How many places in the world can say that?

‘ HOI POLLOI ’

STAMFORD RAFFLES founded two Zoos ; one for animals in Regent’s Park, London, where you will find his bust appropriately enough in the Lion House, and the other for human beings in Singapore, the City of the Lion.

Every ten years, in the year ending with the numeral one, there comes a day when we find a number stuck on our door ; and later on we are given a form which we have to fill up with many details. We then discover in our domains many previously unconsidered trifles, such as the gardener’s grandmother and the cook’s brother’s wife and a friend or two of the head-boy, out of jobs but not above sleeping in the boy’s quarters and enjoying master’s coffee and bread. We have a grand time filling up the form, which we do, as a rule, not too accurately, since we are pretty vague about the religions of our Chinese servants (though much less so than they themselves), and old amah, who quite obviously has long weathered fifty, coyly admits to ‘ perhaps thirty-two,’ while the Malay servants all guess their ages as ‘ more or less ’ whatever it may be.

Time does not mean much to the Asiatic, and he has his own way of reckoning. I once asked a ricksha coolie how long he had been waiting, and he replied, 'Two and a half cigarettes,' which was about as graphic a description of time as I have yet met.

Eventually and laboriously we get our forms filled and they are duly collected. We regard it all as good fun or a damned nuisance, according to the state of our livers, and we forget all about it for another ten years.

Afterwards—long afterwards—the Report of the Superintendent of the Census of Malaya (all capitals, just like that) is duly published, but as it is contained in a book some twelve inches long, eight inches broad, and one and a quarter inches thick, and as the book costs five or six dollars, nobody reads it save a few Government officials, a few journalists, and a very few inquisitive busybodies like myself. The Report soon passes into the blessed nirvana of the Government records, where it collects dust or provides excellent board and lodging for silver-fish.

But the peoples of Malaya have been counted, their ages and habits recorded, and all has been done in seemly British fashion, with a minimum of haste and a maximum of care.

As a matter of actual fact, however, census reports are well worth reading, and are full of curious information such as what that eminent Chinese Commissioner of Customs, the late Mr. Chao Ju-Kua, had to say in A.D. 1225 about Trengganu, what the well-dressed aboriginal lady omits to wear, why Singapore has a climate, how many miles of tarmac road run through the Malay Peninsula, and so on and so forth; nice clean fun!

Let us have a look at the weird mob which fills Singapore, taking our figures from the 1931 census. Altogether there were 567,433 persons then on the island, of whom 447,741 were located within Municipal limits, which means within the town proper; and that town was so thickly over-populated that it ran 14,000 persons to the acre. In one division of Chinatown over 18,000 persons were enumerated within the boundaries of an area under 30 acres, which works out at about one person to a rectangular space of 4 feet by 2 feet! No wonder that Public Enemy No. 1 is Tuberculosis, despite the constant sunshine.

Out of the total population no less than 418,640 were Chinese, which explains why so many people think that Singapore is in China. In fact, China is in Singapore; but at this date a strong bar has been clamped down temporarily on immigration, and it is not likely to be lifted until prosperity has rounded its celebrated corner and is a long way up the next street.

We call all white people ‘ Europeans,’ whether they come from Europe or the United States or Australia, &c. ; and of them in 1931 there were 8147, though to-day there are fewer owing to trade depression. The Europeans included English, Irish, Scottish, Welsh, Australians, New Zealanders, Canadians, Americans, Belgians, Danes, Dutch, French, Germans, Greeks, Italians, Norwegians, Portuguese, Russians, Spaniards, Swedes, Swiss, and ‘ other Europeans ’—of what kind only God and the census officer know, because the latter got too fatigued to tell us.

Sorry to have inflicted that list upon you, but it describes the cosmopolitan nature of this city better than any other way of which I could think.

When you go along our streets and ask your guide or friend who are the different kinds of Asiatics you see, he will probably answer you in very general terms, such as ‘ Oh, that’s a Malay,’ or ‘ That’s a Kling,’ or ‘ That’s a Bengali,’ &c., because we follow the very sweeping generalizations of the Malay language as used locally ; but in reality the business is tremendously complicated.

Thus, what are vaguely called ‘ Malays ’ (numbering 71,177) include actually real Malays, Javanese, Boyanese, Achinese, Bataks, Banjarese, Bugis, Dyaks, and people from Menangkabau, Korinchi, Jambi, Palembang, and elsewhere in

Sumatra, and from Dutch North Borneo and other of the Netherlands Indies.

The 'Klings' include Tamils, Telugus, and Malabaris; the 'Bengalis' include Punjabis, Sikhs, Bengalis proper, Hindustanis, Pathans, Gujeratis, Rajputs, Mahrattas, Parsees, and even Burmese and Gurkhas, besides many other Indian races.

Then, too, we have Arabs, Singhalese, Japanese, Annamites, Armenians, Filipinos, Oriental Jews, Persians, Siamese, and other Asiatic races.

In addition to all the above there are representatives of races whose presence in Singapore is not a little curious. Thus, there are or were quite recently Negroes to be found here, and even an American Indian or two. Myself, I know a coal-black Abyssinian eunuch, a perfectly gorgeous creature who has stepped right out of the *Arabian Nights*. He ought to be armed with a scimitar, but, alas, he is a land-broker nowadays, having long since left the Arab harem which he once adorned. Again, you will see from time to time wild-looking Koreans wandering the streets; and I have occasionally noticed Tibetan monks, presumably on their way to or from China, and unkempt holy men from Northern India in vivid green robes, with great chains of rough amber round their necks. During the mutiny of 1915, weird creatures were caught up in the drag-nets who spoke no translatable language and who came from God knows where.

Singapore has been called the navel of the Malay countries, but it might almost be the navel of Asia.

When you say Chinese, you utter a mouthful. The principal tribes represented in Singapore are the Hok-kiens, Teo-Chius, Khehs, Hok-Chias, Cantonese, Hailams, Hok-Chius, and Kwong-Sais; and do they 'speak Chinese'? No, they do not. You can say correctly enough that a man can read or write Chinese, but no one can say that he speaks it. He can only claim to speak one or more of the languages (or dialects, as they are wrongly called) of China. Between these languages, such as Mandarin, Cantonese, Hok-kien, Teo-chiu, and so forth, there lies as great a difference as there does between European languages, and it is scarcely an exaggeration to say that there are as many different Chinese languages and as many different dialects of those languages as there are languages and dialects in Europe. We have, too, a peculiar kind of Chinese, known as Straits-born, many of whom only speak what is known as Baba Malay, and not a word of any Chinese tongue; they are all British subjects, and have many customs peculiar to themselves.

Imagine, then, what a babel of tongues rises

daily in the streets and buildings of Singapore. In the Law Courts and places where exactitude is essential, an array of interpreters is required; but elsewhere we have one common tongue in which we can communicate, a bastard Malay which makes a *lingua franca* and with which, when all else fails, we can generally make ourselves understood.

Malay is a simple language and very expressive. When anything complicated is necessary, one finds that the word is not Malay but is imported from Sanskrit, Tamil, Persian, Portuguese, or what have you. This illustration will suffice to give you an idea of how the Malay expresses things. *Mata* means an eye; *Mata Hari*, the eye of the day, means the sun; *Mata mata* means the eyes (the plural being expressed by using the singular twice), but it also means a policeman since he is the eyes of government; *Mata mata glap* means secret eyes, and so a detective. I am afraid that much of the Malay spoken by Europeans in Singapore to-day is of the 'Boy, piggy (go) upstairs dan bawa (and bring) my slippers' variety, since English is getting more and more understood every day, and Malay less and less necessary. Even the Hailam servants nowadays speak a language which they allege to be English. Here are three recent specimens from my collection—Flenchy Fleans (French beans); Forky Fie (pork pie), and Weemuster Soss (Worcester

Sauce); but the ricksha coolies still speak no known tongue. If you want to tell them where to go, you grunt hard, then point; if you don't know where the place is, God help you, because the coolie won't. He'll run off somewhere where he thinks you may want to go and grin happily when he finds he's guessed wrong, after which he'll run off somewhere else and grin happily again, and so on until you and your temper are entirely lost. But please don't hit him or kick him as I too often see people doing; he can't help it, and he really is the cheeriest, best-humoured, most hard-working schoolboy of a fellow. And *what* a life!

Just as there are a myriad tongues, so there are a myriad racial customs, for each community remains self-contained and conservative of the habits and thoughts of its home land. I would recommend any stranger who agrees that mankind is the proper study of man to drop into the Police Courts, or the Supreme Court if the criminal assizes are being held. There he will hear the interpreters at work, he will see how carefully justice is done here with absolute equality for all, and he will understand as nowhere else why this place prospers and is contented. He will also, if he is lucky, hear many strange things.

Despite all the outward modernity of Singapore, deep underneath are age-old beliefs and ancient superstitions. The witch-doctor, black magic, and the evil eye still play their part. There is at least one well-known person in Singapore who is supposed to possess occult powers. Here is a true story about him, as I can personally vouch. He once found himself faced with an awkward situation involving an appearance in the Police Court, but he asserted publicly and widely that nobody could bring a case against him. The first prosecuting lawyer was stricken with lumbago and had to go to bed; the next was stricken with blindness which later turned out to be due to teeth; then the principal witness against our friend died; then the next principal witness fell so ill that he nearly died; and then the prosecutor got the wind up and the case fizzled out. Naturally our friend's reputation as a *pawang* (witch-doctor) went aces high.

On one occasion fairly recently I noticed in the Supreme Court a most evil-looking man sitting at the back of the bar table with his eyes fixed on the empty seat where the Judge was about to appear. I asked who he was, and was told by a lawyer's clerk, 'Oh, he's a *pawang* come to bewitch the Judge; but it's all right, he's on our side.'

In a very well-known murder case which occurred a good many years ago, the prosecution was in need of oral evidence, so two Javanese grass-cutters were taken to a *pawang* who persuaded them into the belief that they had seen some very strange occurrences, which they duly related with vivid detail. Unfortunately it was discovered later that they had been somewhere else at the time, and they were duly sentenced for perjury. When the committing magistrate asked them if they had any witnesses whom they wanted to be summoned at the Assizes, one of them replied, 'No, but if I had known this was going to happen, I would have had'!

I once saw a crowd collected outside a Police Court up-country, and, asking what it was all about, was told that they were waiting for a monkey to give evidence! It appeared that the police had taken away a monkey which was the sole living thing on the scene of a murder. They could not, of course, leave him there to starve, but the gentle villagers had got the idea that a local *pawang* had made the monkey tell the story of the crime, and the crowd outside the Court had come to hear the monkey do his stuff!

With all the mingling of races in Singapore there is but little assimilation or mixture of blood. The Eurasians, as we call those of mixed white and Asiatic blood are very self-contained, and have their own culture and their own traditions; their population increases by natural causes and very little by new mixtures. The different kinds of Malays are Mohammedans, and intermingle to a good extent among themselves but not much with Mohammedan Indians. The rest keep mostly within their own communities, since nearly all are immigrants, come here to shake the golden pagoda tree, gather up the fruit, and depart to their own home lands. Very few comparatively, either Asiatic or white, start with any permanent intention to settle; but yearly the domiciled communities are increasing rapidly, and this will be more and more so as the years pass, because the old days of easy money and quick fortunes have gone for ever. It is principally with these domiciled people that in my view the future of Singapore will be found to lie, and each year their problem becomes more important to our Government. But even though our peoples are so largely immigrant, there has always been a strong spirit of citizenship here, especially amongst the white peoples and the educated Asiatics, so that, paraphrasing a well-known French saying, one can observe with truth that here a man has two countries, his own and Singapore.

From a social point of view our greatest weakness lies in the marked disproportion of the males over the females amongst many races, particularly the white ones and the Chinese. The problem of prostitution accordingly presents many difficulties.

Pardon the introduction of so unpleasant a subject, but you can help us greatly by understanding our problem and by spreading that understanding. The young white man in Singapore runs a most ghastly danger which it is utterly unfair to put in his way. Financial reasons usually prevent him from making an early marriage, in addition to which most employers set their faces resolutely against marriage before a certain income has been reached. He has, moreover, no home life here; there is no easy companionship between the sexes and, when he does meet white women, it is rarely under conditions that are entirely normal. So sex, which presents a big enough problem to the unmarried man in his own country, assumes here an exaggerated and abnormal aspect. Our European *maisons tolerées*, which used to play a very essential part behind the scenes of the white settlements in the Orient, were all closed during the Great War, principally owing to the fact that their inhabitants were almost all of enemy nationality. Not only have they never been reopened, but since 1930 a rigid campaign of suppression has been forced upon us by enthusiasts in England and elsewhere, so that white prostitutes have been driven away entirely, and brothels of all kinds have been closed down. But unfortunately you cannot close down human nature.

The result has been sly prostitution and widespread venereal disease, ruined careers, and broken health, a terrible price to pay for moral enthusiasms. A dreadful mistake has been made, and it is high time that our own doctors, police officers, and legislators were left to deal with matters in the light of local conditions which only they can properly appreciate. The report of the Municipal Health Officer for 1932 as to syphilis is as disquieting a document as I have ever read : and any old hand amongst the doctors will tell you why and what is to blame.

And now let us turn to a wholly pleasant aspect of our social life, the great part which athletics play to-day in the lives of Europeans and Asiatics. Go round Singapore any fine afternoon and you cannot but be struck by the numbers of playing-fields filled with enthusiasts. I doubt if the English can point to anything that they have done here which has been more to the good of their Asiatic fellow-citizens than the teaching of games and good sportsmanship. With the Asiatics the favourite sports are cricket, Association football, swimming, basketball, badminton, tennis, and boxing. Their women, too, are beginning to take up games freely. The general result has been a marked improvement in the physique and morale of our Asiatics, and I know of no sign that points more to a fine future for this town than the new spirit which athletics have introduced. It is only old hands like myself who can truly realize the wonderful change which has come over the life of the city, for we remember the days when not an Asiatic played anything but *sepak raga*, a Malay game in which a wicker ball is kept in the air by kicking it from player to player.

THE FORBIDDEN HILL

SINGAPORE is, roughly speaking, a diamond-shaped island, the points of which are set north and south, west and east. The town itself lies on either side of the Singapore River, and its heart beats in the bowl of that river, its spine being formed by a road which is pedantically called, on one side of the river, North Bridge Road and, on the other, South Bridge Road, since it crosses the river, which runs from west to east, at Elgin Bridge. From the heart of the town the main arterial roads branch out fan-wise, covering the most part of the island.

In the centre the town huddles and snuggles and tumbles over itself. As it reaches farther out, it runs north to Tanglin, the principal European residential quarter; to the east and west it spatters out through coco-nut groves and rubber trees to the seaside residences of Tanjong Katong (Turtle Point) and Pasir Panjang (Long Sands), but before either of these suburbs is reached one passes through industrial areas. That to the west is in process of creation, though already you will find there brick-works, rubber-works, and two new breweries; that to the east, in the basin of the Kallang River, is nearly fully developed with rubber-works, foundries, saw-mills, gas-works, and other things as smelly as numerous.

Peering short-sightedly over the roofs of Singapore from the middle of the town there is a squat little hill—squat because long since it had its top lopped off and flattened out. It is called Fort Canning, and it is where the military have their headquarters, and frequently wrack one's nerves by loosing off their saluting guns. Upon the hill there are also a lighthouse, very important to navigators, and a signalling staff the flags on which, if you are wise in such matters, will tell you what ships are making port. I do not suppose that any one ever gives this little hill a second thought; it is just there and very familiar. Yet, as a matter of fact, it is an intensely interesting little hill, around which one could write the history of Singapore, and it has known at least three important phases of existence—the first when it was called Forbidden Hill, the next when it was Government Hill, and the last, and present, when it became Fort Canning.

Of its first phase, there remain at this date only an ancient tomb, some gold jewellery, and a fragment of inscribed rock; of its second, a very pathetic cemetery where repose the remains of the first Christians to be buried here, among whom are a few Americans ; of its third, all else that you see to-day.

The first phase relates, of course, to ancient Singhapura, concerning the origin of which you will read in the piece I call 'The Old Man of the Mountain.' This ancient city had a history of about one hundred years from somewhere about the middle of the thirteenth century A.D. to the middle of the fourteenth, and was ruled over by five kings in all, according to the Malay Annals.

These kings had their palace on the top of Fort Canning, to which they forbade the populace to ascend; hence its old Malay name, *Bukit Larangan*, meaning the Forbidden Hill. Behind it was a clear stream that was called the Forbidden Stream, because the ladies of the royal household went there to bathe. After their arrival in 1819, the British cleared this hill and found that the greater part of its western and northern sides were covered with the remains of the foundations of buildings, some of which were composed of baked brick of good quality. The largest of these ruins was on a terrace about forty feet square, and would seem to have formed the King's palace or perhaps a temple. There was another terrace on the north side where there was a tomb, which you can see to-day, and which was said in 1822 to have been that of Iskandar Shah, the last king of Singapore, and founder

FORT CANNING, SINGAPORE

THE TOMB OF ISKANDAR SHAH, SINGAPORE

of the Malacca Sultanate ; hence the name which you will see at the head of the tomb.

Among the ruins were found various descriptions of pottery, both Chinese and native, together with Chinese brass coins of the tenth and eleventh centuries, the earliest being dated A.D. 967 and the latest A.D. 1085. These dates, of course, prove nothing, because such coins remained in circulation in Malaysia for centuries after their original importation. All these things have long since disappeared, but during excavations in 1928 some ancient gold jewellery was found about 120 yards from the tomb of Iskandar Shah. It is Indian work, and seems to date from the fourteenth century ; you can see it in Raffles Museum.

The ancient town of Singhapura extended from the hill to the Singapore River on one side, and on the other to what is Stamford Canal to-day ; to these boundaries the hill was joined on each side by walls about a mile long. These walls were sixteen feet in breadth at their base and about ten feet high, and the hill was further protected by salt marshes and streams at its feet, while a moat ran round the part where the king's buildings stood.

Though small according to modern ideas, the town must have been a considerable place for those times. The *Commentaries* of Albuquerque, the great Portuguese viceroy who captured

Malacca in 1511, say that 'Singapore was a big town with a large population, as is evidenced by the large ruins which one sees there to-day.' Barros, who accompanied Albuquerque as official historian, says that ancient 'Singapore was an emporium where all the ships went as to a general emporium, to a world fair; for some it was the end of the eastern sea, for others, of the western'; and as an emporium with free trade for all it was refounded by Stamford Raffles and remains to-day.

The ancient Portuguese writers also say that Singhapura was Ptolemy's Zaba; and for my part I believe that it was the place to which Marco Polo referred as Malaiur, but which incidentally he never visited.

Singhapura fell somewhere about A.D. 1360, when the Javanese conquered it. Its king and the remnant of his followers were driven out after scenes of destruction and bloodshed, the tragic memory of which still haunts Malay tradition. The hill was for long (and maybe still is) supposed to be haunted by the ghosts of its dead kings and queens; and I myself remember some twenty-five years ago, when the Royal Artillery Mess used to be on Fort Canning, and sounds of revelry were to be heard on the hill by night, that my Malay *sais* (coachman) would never drive me up after dark or fetch me back in the small hours of the morning. I had either to spend the night there, where it was always delightfully cool and sometimes cold, or hire me a toothless ancient who drove a four-wheeled roofed-in contraption called a gharry, with a broken-winded piebald Deli pony. Neither he nor the pony feared anything save, respectively, missing a fare or a feed.

The tombs of the ancient kings and queens were still on the hill after the British came, but what happened to them I do not know, for to-day the only one remaining is that of Iskandar Shah. If you are interested to see it, go into the old European cemetery through the main gate, follow the path that leads straight up, and turn to the left. The tree that grows over the tomb is alone worth the visit, and the little bridge to it passes over the old moat that once surrounded and protected the king's palace; but don't pay any attention to what you are told by the old caretaker. He is as vague and unreliable as all his kind, and lamentably ignorant about his charge, which incidentally was also that of his father and his grandfather. The tomb is known locally as the *Kramat*, meaning holy place, and has plenty of devotees.

The last relic of ancient Singhapura is the fragment of inscribed stone in Raffles Museum. It was part of a large rock which stood on the point of the right bank of the river at its mouth, but which was blown up long ago by Government engineers. In 1819 this point was covered with forest trees and jungle. While this was being cleared some Indian sailors brought to notice a big rock of unhewn sandstone which had split in the centre. On the insides of the two pieces were ancient inscriptions. The sailors were so terrified that they refused to clear any further, and Chinese coolies had to be hired at high wages.

Though a fairly good tracing of the remains of this inscription were made by a naval officer, and though good tracings were also made of three pieces of the rock that went to the Calcutta Museum, nobody has yet succeeded in reading one word of it. The wise men, however, agree that the writing is the ancient Javanese script called Kawi; and it may be, if that is so, that the Javanese who destroyed Singhapura made the inscription to record their victory. The Malay Annals contain an interesting legend about the rock which concerns their mythical strong man Badang, and this is the story:

There was a man at Salwang in Johore who had a slave named Badang. One day this latter set a snare to catch fish, and next morning found none, only scales and bones. This continued to happen for several mornings, so Badang hid and kept watch by the snare.

He saw an *hantu* (in this sense Jinn) come to eat the fish. 'His eyes were red as fire, his hair coarse and matted as a basket, his beard hanging down to his navel, and in his hand a whittle knife without the haft'—a truly unpleasant customer, but Badang was not perturbed. He seized the *hantu*, and it was the latter who became frightened, saying 'Pray, don't kill me, and I will give you any gift you like.' Badang thought to himself, 'If I should desire riches, they would all belong to my master; or if I should ask the gift of invisibility, I might nevertheless die; but if in like manner I were to ask for strength to perform my master's business—yes, truly that would be of some advantage to me.' So Badang philosophically asked for strength, and the *hantu* gave it to him; and, trying it, Badang found that he could shiver trees to pieces with the greatest ease.

News of his strength duly reached Singapore, and the king sent for Badang, appointed him a prince, and after several marvels Badang became the local king's champion. The King of Kalinga in southern India, hearing of Badang's prowess, sent down his own champion to wrestle with him, and bet seven ships on his man. The tussle began, and Badang seemed always to have the advantage. Now, there was a huge stone lying before the king's palace, and the Indian champion said, 'Let us try our strength. Let him be reckoned worse who cannot lift this stone.'

The Indian lifted it as high as his knee and then let it fall; but Badang took it up, poised it easily, and threw it into the mouth of the river, 'where it is still visible,' say the Malay Annals, written in A.D. 1612.

It is an extraordinary thing that you cannot go into a bookseller's in Singapore and buy an English translation of the Malay Annals, or the Story of Abdullah, or the Story of Hang-Tuah, or any other of the well-known Malay works. They appear to be kept as a holy hunting-ground for our pundits. This is very foolish, for they are very good reading and would sell well. As the Malay story-tellers say, it can be said of each of them that it is 'a tale composed by men of old, a beautiful tale, the very music of which is enough to flood the heart with tender recollections.'

After the sack of Singhapura, there are various references to the island and its straits during the succeeding centuries. For some time, at all events, there was a Malay harbour-master with an office on the island, and there seems at another time to have been a commander of the island under the old Sultans of Malacca, but it is only as a port of call that the place appears generally. In 1811 Johore Malays, under a chief called the Temenggong, settled on the island near the mouth of the river, and there Stamford Raffles found them when he landed during the evening of January 28, 1819. His ships, six in number, anchored off the present Quarantine Island called St. John's. The Malays at that time called this island *Si Kijang*, or 'the roe,' and the name was converted by English sailors, who did not understand the Malay, into St. John's, just as they converted so many other names, a classic instance of which is the well-known Junkceylon from Ujong Salang. On St. John's Island to-day stands our Quarantine Station, said by experts to be one of the finest in the world.

From the Temenggong and from the then Sultan of Johore, Raffles took a lease of a portion of the island on behalf of the East India Company. Everything was done (as it so often is) by superior officers to kill the new settlement and stamp out the whole enterprise, but fortunately their efforts failed, and in 1824 the island was bought outright; so we pass to the second phase of our little hill.

Here it is, now called Government Hill, and we see the top laid out in a beautiful garden with a big wooden bungalow, with venetians and an attap-thatch roof, consisting of two parallel halls with front and back verandas, terminated by two square wings which comprised the sleeping apartments. This was Government House, for long the centre of social activity in Singapore, and the scene of great doings during the three years 1839 to 1842, when Singapore was the base for the Opium War with China which led to the founding of Hong-Kong in 1841. The ancients of Singapore were magnificent trenchermen, and descriptions of their dinner parties are truly gargantuan, obviously accounting for a great deal of the ill-health which gradually got the place a bad name. One old description of a dinner party tells us that it began with different soups in silver tureens, mock-turtle and mulligatawny being the favourites. Soup over, the host asked his leading lady guest to take wine, an example followed with alacrity by all the other guests. Fish, then joints of sweet Bengal mutton, Chinese capons, Kedah fowls and Sangora ducks, Yorkshire hams, Java potatoes, and Malay ubis followed. The ladies unbent from their dignity, and a general round of drinking healths occurred, during which the table was cleared and the next course succeeded, a short one of curry and rice, accompanied with sambals of pungent taste, Bombay ducks and campar roes, salted turtle eggs, and omelettes. To wash the curry down, pale ale was served. The servants cleared the table once more, and the dessert followed, macaroni puddings, shapes, and custards, during which champagne flowed freely. After this, a huge cheese was placed on the table, which was discussed with more pale ale. The writer naively remarks that by that time a rosy pink bloomed on the cheeks of the climate-worn, wan, and pale ladies! But still

GOVERNMENT HILL, SINGAPORE, 1840

HIGH JINKS IN 1854

THE OLD ASSEMBLY ROOMS, SINGAPORE

they had not had enough, for the table was cleared of its cloth and numerous fruits with wine were placed upon it. These same ancient settlers for years used to get up at five in the morning to the call of a saluting gun, after which they went out walking for an hour to two hours, and considered this the best way of keeping their health.

In the old Government House there occurred one of the dramatic moments of British history. On Sunday, May 31, 1857, the opium steamer *Fiery Cross* came into Singapore from Calcutta, and she brought disastrous news. The Sepoys had mutinied at Meerut and the revolt was spreading fast. Three days later the eighth Earl of Elgin disembarked in Singapore. He had been appointed British Plenipotentiary in China, and was expecting a man-o'-war to take him from Singapore to that country. By the grace of God there was at this time a British expeditionary force approaching Singapore on its way to take military action against the Chinese, and, when Lord Elgin heard the bad news from India, he considered at once the diversion of this expedition to India.

Naturally, he was staying at Government House, and there all night he paced up and down the long veranda interviewing the Governor, Mr. Blundell, who was an old Indian official, and the senior naval and military officers who were waiting the arrival of the Expeditionary Force. It was a fateful decision for Lord Elgin. If he misjudged the seriousness of the Indian situation and unnecessarily diverted the troops, he was a broken man. If, on the other hand, he let the troops go on to China, India might be lost to the British. At long last he made his decision. As dawn broke, a steamer was dispatched to the Straits of Sunda and the troops were ordered to India, which by that order was saved to the British Empire.

The defence of Singapore has caused England much perturbation from time to time. In the 'fifties there was a thorough overhaul of these defences, with the result that Government House was removed in 1859 and the Hill was converted into Fort Canning. The top of it was levelled off and seven 68-pounders were put in position facing the sea. When the work was finished, it was noticed that Pearl's Hill, where the gaol is to-day, was higher; so the military engineers had to cut down the top of that hill! At the same time as Fort Canning was being constructed, Fort Fullerton at the mouth of the river, where Fullerton Building containing the General Post Office stands to-day, was also enlarged and strongly armed. The Battery Road of to-day was originally so called because it led to the battery which preceded Fort Fullerton.

And to-day the defences of Singapore are still causing perturbation, as is evidenced by the new naval base and aerial defences. The British are busily engaged in building up their defensive works, and the Japanese are busily engaged in exporting from the Malay Peninsula hundreds of thousands of tons of the world's finest iron-ore, of wolfram and manganese, while Mars, Siva, Kuan-Ti, and the other gods of destruction must be enjoying what Hollywood rudely calls a belly laugh.

The Governor, evicted from the Hill, went first to Oxley Estate, where he occupied the Pavilion; and the present Government House was opened in 1869, very much then as it still is, though additions have been made.

Fort Canning long ago ceased to be a fort, and to-day is Military Headquarters for the Singapore command; but the little hill continues to look out over the same old sea with its eleven thousand islands (count them) and, like other philosophers, doubtless ruminates over the strange mutability of human affairs.

MANY GODS

IN Singapore we worship many gods, hold many religious festivals, have several New Year's Days, use several different calendars, and keep our accounts in quite a few strange ways, the oldest being on palm-leaves, a practice still in use among some of our Indian money-lenders. In any Chinese shop you will see and hear the oldest known calculating machine, the abacus, a frame with a number of parallel wire rods divided unequally by a transverse bar of wood. On each rod are seven balls, five on one side of the dividing bar and two on the other, and they are shifted rapidly up and down as the calculation proceeds, giving out a very merry clicking noise. You can generally get a good idea of trade conditions by walking slowly along any street where there are large Chinese business houses and listening for the clicks of the abacus. If you hear them like crickets in the jungle, all is well; but nowadays there are ominous silences.

Every major religion is represented here, and almost every major sect of that religion; and I would like to tell you a little about these religions.

The followers of Christ have their appointed places of worship, the oldest of which is the little Armenian Church in Hill Street, built in 1835. The Church of England has its St. Andrew's Cathedral, designed on the lines of Netley Abbey in England, by Colonel Macpherson, the Colonial Engineer of those days. It was built by Indian convicts to the glory of a God they did not know, which may account for the cheerlessness of its interior, and it was completed in 1862, having taken six years to build. Then there are the French Catholic Church of the Good Shepherd, dating from 1843; the Portuguese Catholic Cathedral, where a most interesting kind of passion play is enacted on Good Fridays; and the Presbyterian, Methodist, Baptist, Seventh-Day Adventist, Christian Science, and several other places of Christian worship; but most pleasant of them all is the peaceful French convent. Go into this last and a feeling of security and peace will descend upon you, with a vast respect for the courage and self-sacrifice of the quiet nuns, of whom only a very, very few have ever returned to their beautiful France. In the Convent unwanted babies of all races are left and are cared for; there little girls of every nationality are educated, and splendidly educated; and there, if anywhere in Singapore, the gentle spirit of the Holy Infant Jesus breathes and invigorates. Myself, I am Church of England and spent my schooldays beneath the spires of Canterbury Cathedral at the ancient King's School, but I am happy to express what a tremendous debt Singapore owes to the little ladies of the Convent.

The oldest Christian Churches in Malaya are, of course, to be found in Malacca. On top of the hill there stand the remains of the Church of Our Lady of the Mount, built by the great Albuquerque shortly after his conquest of Malacca in 1511; but the oldest Christian Church still in daily use is that of St. Peter, in Bunga Raya, Malacca, built in 1608, and containing a contemporary figure of Christ that is carried round the town each year. In Malacca, too, is the tomb of Bishop Peter of the Jesuit Society, the second Bishop of Japan, who died in the Straits of Singapore in 1598, and the town is permeated by the memories of the great St. Francis Xavier, the patron of all those Catholics who work for the salvation of infidels.

Let us now turn to the Asiatic religions and their places of worship.

As you drive along the roads in the country you will often notice a giant tree rising in lonely splendour, and sometimes you will see at its feet a kind of shrine with red-and-white flags and burning candles or papers. It is *kramat* (holy), and all kinds of Asiatics, principally women, are apt to worship there although they

THE GREAT SULTAN MOSQUE, SINGAPORE
FROM BUSSORAH STREET

THE CHETTIAR TEMPLE, SINGAPORE

have their own proper gods elsewhere. Here one sees the survival of one of man's oldest forms of devotion, tree-worship, and around such trees there is a lot of secret belief that is very hard, almost impossible, to discover accurately. There are also to be seen many solitary trees to which not a man, Malay, Indian, or Chinese, will lay an axe; they are inhabited by some *hantu* (ghost), but try your hardest to find out why this is believed and you will get just nowhere: you don't belong.

The principal place of Mohammedan worship in Singapore is the fine Sultan Mosque in North Bridge Road, designed by Mr. Denis Santry, but unfortunately it is so surrounded by houses that its artistic merits are hard to appreciate. The best way to see it is from the back at the top of Bussorah Street, and the best time is at sunset or on a moonlight night. It is then a very beautiful sight, and collects around it the most lovely blue shadows. The principal Mohammedan festivals in Singapore are the Moharram or *Hari Raya Puasa*, as the Malays call it, which begins the new year and concludes the *bulan puasa* or fasting month. In the following month, Safar, there is a day when the Malays put on their prettiest clothes and go to the seaside to feast and to bathe. There is no happier or brighter person than a Malay dressed up in his best and bent on holiday-making. Lastly, there is the *Hari Raya Haji*, at the end of the Mohammedan year, and this is a festival principally for those who wear the white cap signifying that they are Hajis, that is, those who have made the pilgrimage to Mecca ; but all take part in it.

Those Indians who are not Mohammedans follow the Brahman or Hindu religion, and their principal places of worship are the Chettiar Temple in Tank Road, and the Mariamman Temple in South Bridge Road. The latter is the older, having been built by Indian convicts in the early decades of last century. The Tank Road temple is, however, much the finer, and well worth a visit. Founded more than seventy years ago, it belongs to the Singapore Chettiars, who are a caste of southern Indians, being traders, bankers, and money-lenders, and coming from the Nattukottai district of the Madras Presidency. Great wealth has been poured into this temple and its endowments, and amongst its treasures, which you will see, are two silver chariots from 20 to 22 feet in height, a golden peacock adorned with jewels on festival days, a silver peacock, and the equestrian statues of Hindu deities mounted in gold and silver. The temple is open to visitors at any time during the day, and they will be shown courteously all that is to be seen. The great festival at this temple occurs during Taipusam, the occasion when Subramanian, the particular god of the

Chettiars, revealed himself to his devotees riding on a peacock. During this festival, which occurs in January or February usually, the god Subramanian is taken round the town in solemn procession in the large silver car, drawn by two sacred white buffaloes, and a great reception is held at the temple to which all are welcome, whatever their race or creed, while the devotees are fed in the courtyard from huge cauldrons of rice and curry, which they pile up on fresh banana-leaves, and from the over-eating of which most of them pass into a coma.

During the Taipusam festival one sees some dreadful sights, since that is one of the times when devotees perform acts of self-torture as the result of vows made in times of calamity during the preceding year. Another such time is at the fire-walking ceremony, which occurs usually at the end of October, in the Mariamman Temple. The popular Hindu conception of man's duty to the gods and the manner of discharging it consists in lifting the *Kavadi*, wearing spikes, walking on fire, and such self-tortures. The gods are generally to be propitiated by mortifying the flesh and so exalting the soul. At the back of these things, which seem so unnecessarily dreadful to European eyes, there lies, then, a very fine spiritual idea which, however, is unknown to the bulk of the ignorant Tamil population who do these things. There is, however, a further medical aspect, for from time immemorial the Hindus have believed in the efficacy of bleeding and scorching certain parts of the body to cure and remedy serious physical maladies and defects.

Finally, there is a third great Hindu festival in Singapore called Tivavali in Tamil, a festival of joy, which falls at the end of October or the beginning of November.

Travelling in South-Eastern Asia you will see much of Brahmanism. Its trinity consists of Brahma the Creator, Vishnu the Preserver, and Siva the Destroyer. Amongst the other of its best known deities in our part of the world are Parvati, Siva's wife; Ganesha, their son, the god of knowledge, portrayed with an elephant's head; Kuvera, the god of riches; Rama, the hero and central figure of the great Hindu epic called the Ramayana; and Kama, the god of love. With the Hindu gods are associated mythological animals and birds, the most important of which is the Nandi or bull, upon which Siva rides, the finest specimen of which in Malaysia you will see in the great Hindu temple at Prambanan, in Java. You will notice how worn is its nose, and it will interest you to know that this wearing has been caused by the stomachs of thousands of women of all races and creeds, since it is said that by rubbing their stomachs on the Nandi they will become fruitful. Then there is the Garuda, the great bird of Vishnu, which you will see so often. In Bali they make superbly coloured Garudas which are highly decorative. Put one in a room and it will dominate everything else. The Makara, a fabulous sea animal, is another curious Hindu figure of mythology, an ancient specimen of which is to be seen in Malacca, on the wall near the Stadt-house. And, finally, there is the Naga, or hooded cobra with seven heads, which plays a considerable part in the Hindu mythology, but which in South-Eastern Asia is most frequently found in conjunction with Buddhism, that religion having borrowed much from Brahmanism. At Angkor Vat you will see much of the Naga; and many of the small effigies of Buddha, which are still purchasable, show him in conjunction with it.

And that takes me to the religions and customs of the Chinese.

Buddhism was born on the banks of the holy river Ganges, its founder being an Indian prince, Sakyamuni, commonly called Gautama Buddha, who lived from 563 to 483 B.C., according to the opinion prevalent to-day. The religion which he founded flourished in India until the fifth century A.D., when it was overwhelmed by Brahmanism; but long before then southern Indians had carried the religion into South-Eastern Asia, and it had also been carried into

China, whence it spread to Japan. Buddhism was essentially an international religion, which explains how it was that in its home land it was destroyed by the intensely nationalistic Brahmanism, whilst outside that home land it continued to flourish and still is the dominant religion in Tibet, Ceylon, Burma, Siam, Indo-China, China, and Japan.

It is usually said that the religions of China are three: Buddhism, Confucianism, and Taoism. As we have seen, the first was founded by Gautama Buddha; the second was founded by Confucius, or, to give him his Chinese name, Kung Fu Tzu, who was born in 551 B.C.; and the last was founded by Lao Tzu, who was born not long before Confucius. The middle of the sixth century before Christ was a striking period in the history of human thought. In Greece it produced Socrates, Plato, and Aristotle; in Persia, Zoroaster; in India, Gautama Buddha; and in China, Confucius and Lao Tzu.

But though the religions of China are three, the people neither practise all three together nor any one of them separately, for a popular religion has taken shape through the ages; yet all three have their separate clergy—the Buddhists their bonzes, the Taoists their monks and sorcerers, and for the official religion (usually but wrongly called Confucianism) functionaries of all ranks.

HINDU DEVOTEE CARRYING THE KAVADI

THE SPIKED ENDS PIERCE HIS FLESH

THE OLDEST CHINESE TEMPLE IN MALAYA

THE CHENG HOON TENG TEMPLE, MALACCA

THE KEK LOK MONASTERY, PENANG

Many and wonderful are the gods of China and far too numerous to mention, but a reference to a very few of them may be useful, and I may remark that it is very hard indeed to find a Chinese who can tell you intelligently about the temples you visit or the gods and goddesses in those temples. Best known of all the gods to tourists in the Orient is Pu-Tai, the so-called laughing Buddha, whose cheery fat-bellied effigy is to be seen everywhere. He is popularly supposed to be an incarnation of Maitreya, the Merciful One, Buddha of the Future, and is the embodiment of carnal virtues, though revered as the Saviour of the World three thousand years hence. Then there is the lovely female figure known as Kuan Yin, the Goddess of Mercy, a kind of Virgin Mary and particularly the Protectress of the Southern Seas, as the Chinese call Malaysia, since she is the patroness of all seamen and travellers. Her effigy is carried in all the sea-going junks, and daily prayers are offered to it by the sailors. She occupies a position that is unique in Chinese eyes and possesses a very beautiful name, 'She Who Looks Down and Hears the Cries of the World,' from which you can easily see the nature of the mythology collected around her. Another sea-goddess is Ma-Cho-Po, who is specially worshipped in the province of Fukien, whence have always come the majority of Chinese sailors and traders in the Southern Seas and of immigrants into Singapore.

Then there are the Eight Immortals, all of whom have their peculiar symbol. They are a band of roysterers, and a purely secular invention; they attained the highest bliss by devious ways of grotesque adventure, aided principally by the magic Elixir of Life. The stories about them are many, mostly of humorous type, and they seem to have arisen out of the revulsion of the man in the street from the pedantic officialdom of the Sung Dynasty.

The principal Chinese temples in Singapore are the Hok-kien temple in Teluk Ayer Street, called Tean Hock Kiong (Lucky Heaven Temple); the Cantonese temple also in Teluk Ayer Street, called Fook Tak Shee (Lucky Shrine); the Teo-Chiu temple in Phillip Street, called Low Yah Kheng (Goddess Temple); the Siong Lim See (Double Jungle Temple) at Kim Keat Road, off the Balestier Road; and the Haw Par Buddhist temple at Racecourse Road.

All are worthy of a visit, but the most interesting are the Hok-kien temple in Teluk Ayer Street, and the temples in Kim Keat Road and Racecourse Road. The first is dedicated to the goddess Ma-Cho-Po, whose effigy you will find in the front shrine. It was brought from Fukien, and was placed on its altar in 1840 by the Fukien traders who built the temple. Back of her shrine is that of Kuan Yin, the temple thus enshrining both the sea-goddesses, and so being a most fitting one for Singapore. The temple in Balestier Road was built and endowed by a wealthy Singapore merchant named Low Kim Pong, and was most ornately adorned, but unfortunately it has not been kept up well since its founder's death. It contains several large Siamese Buddhas and a particularly good Kuan Yin, besides a long series of pictures representing the Buddhist Hells, in all of which the painter has taken a sadistic relish. The Racecourse Road temple is quite new, but contains a huge white marble Buddha. The major cost of building this temple was contributed by Aw Boon Haw and his brother Aw Boon Par, the proprietors of the well-known Tiger Balm, which you will see advertised all over Singapore and, indeed, Malaysia; it is an excellent counter-irritant for headaches and rheumatism, and from it the brothers, who are very modern in their business methods, have amassed a fortune, large parts of which they distribute to philanthropic and religious causes.

The finest Chinese place of worship in Malaya is, however, the great Kek Lok temple and monastery in Penang, at Ayer Hitam; it is said, indeed, to be finer than any in China at present. I once witnessed the performance of a kind of High Mass in this temple, which will always live in my memory. The unusual nature of the ceremony, the serene peace of the chief priest's face, the beauty of movement in his every gesture, and the marvellous red, orange, and yellow robes of the various grades of priests, all presented a picture that was most moving.

But by far the most interesting of all Malayan temples is the ancient Cheng Hoon Teng, or Bright Cloud Pavilion, in Malacca. It was first established by a Buddhist monk, and was then a very small temple surrounded by a garden. It so remained until the beginning of the seventeenth century, when the second Chinese Captain of Malacca, Li Kap, decided to rebuild it; but he died before the work could be undertaken, and his son-in-law, Chan Lak Koa, rebuilt the temple in the early years of the seventeenth century during the period of transition between the Ming and Ching Dynasties. In a chapel at the back of the temple there are the family tablets of the early Chinese Captains of Malacca and other tablets of ancient families no longer in existence, together with a perfectly wonderful Chinese painting of Li Kap in Ming mandarin robes, the blue of which is that heavenly shade which collectors of porcelain know as Mohammedan blue, a colour that has never been approached anywhere else in the world, and the secret of which died shortly after the Ming Dynasty. In that same chapel you will also see two small figures, representing Chan Lak Koa and his wife. The temple is dedicated to Kuan Yin, and there is a very ancient bronze image of the goddess on the main altar.

There are six great Chinese festivals, three for the living and three for the dead. Of the former, the first is the New Year, which usually falls at the end of January or beginning of February. This festival is, of course, still kept up in Singapore, though nothing like as much as in the old days when the Chinese really made whoopee and open house was kept throughout the city, with the Chinese streets beautifully decorated and with much feasting and giving of presents. The second of the festivals for the living is the Dragon-boat Festival in the fifth or Dragon Moon, but this is very mild indeed, in Singapore, with no procession. The last, however, of the festivals for the living is a very popular one here. It is the Harvest Moon Festival, and falls in the eighth or Kindly Moon, being performed when the moon is at its height. The Chinese streets are gay with moon-cakes and coloured lanterns, and even the poorest make some little show.

The first of the three festivals for the dead occurs in the third or Sleepy Moon, and is the day when it is permissible to repair and clean up the tombs. The basis of all Chinese social organization and private life is the family; and ancestor-worship (which Herbert Spencer has said is the root of all religions) may be said to be their principal religion. If you look through the door of any Chinese house in Singapore you will see a long blackwood table in the front hall, beautifully decorated, with porcelain vases, joss-sticks, and candles upon it. That is the family altar, where is kept the *sin-chew* tablet, before which at specified times the family must worship. The word *sin-chew* means the spirit ruler or spiritual head of the family. When the family dies out or becomes too poor to keep up the rites, the tablets are put in a temple for preservation; you will see plenty of them in any temple you visit.

Out of this ancestor-worship rise all Chinese family customs and family law, in particular the customs of polygamy and adoption, designed primarily for the creation of many descendants to keep up and perform the necessary rites for the dead.

The seventh or Moon of Hungry Ghosts is the special month for the dead; it is called locally the *Sembayang Hantu* (Praying to the Ghosts), and on the fifteenth of the moon is the Chinese All Soul's Day. A Chinese cemetery is a wonderful sight on that day. Round the graves you will see the various families placing in front of their ancestors offerings of food with paper reproductions of money, clothing, conveyances, and furniture, the papers being

PREPARING FOR THE WANGKANG FESTIVAL AT MALAÇCA

A STREET IN CHINATOWN, SINGAPORE

burned in order that their ethereal counterparts may reach the hungry ghosts.

In the seventh moon, too, there is a festival with a beautiful idea behind it, when the Weaving Lady and her lover the Cowherd meet in the sky. They are identified with two stars (Aquila and Lyra), one on either side of the Milky Way, which the Chinese call the Silver Stream of Heaven. The Weaving Lady was one of seven spinsters, the daughters of the Kitchen god; and her spirit and those of her sisters are worshipped on the night of the seventh day of the seventh moon by young unmarried girls.

The last of the festivals for the dead is a repetition of the first, and occurs on the first of the tenth or Kindly Moon, during which the ceremony of Burning the Clothes is performed in the houses. The object of this ceremony is to provide clothing for the dead, and once more papers, representing the necessary garments, are burned.

You will have seen from the above that each Chinese moon has its appropriate name; and besides those I have mentioned, the most interesting of these names are the Budding Moon for the second, which in China marks the beginning of spring; the Lotus or sixth moon; the Chrysanthemum or ninth moon; and the Bitter or twelfth moon, when winter fastens a cruel hand on China. Each moon has appropriate festivals, but it is not possible to go into them all here.

Amongst our local festivals are two very interesting ones. The first is the great Ching Gay festival, performed in Penang in the eleventh or White Moon. It is celebrated annually with a huge procession intended to take away sickness and drive away the devils, and usually occurs about the beginning of December. The other is the Wang Kang festival, which occurs once every fifteen years, Chinese reckoning, in Malacca, and which has much the same purpose as the Ching Gay, but which is also intended to ensure Malacca's prosperity for the ensuing fifteen years. It is just about to be performed as I write this in the middle of October. Wang Kang in Chinese means what we call a junk, and the Malacca Chinese make an old-fashioned war junk about the size of an ordinary sampan, and ornament it with gold, silks, and jewels. This they drag in procession round the town and finally burn; they used to fire it and set it out to sea, but this has been stopped because of the danger to navigation. It is all done in honour of the Five Ong Yahs, or Princes, who are somewhat obscure persons in Chinese mythology, but much worshipped by Ho-kiens, who introduced the cult into Malacca, the prosperity of which is believed by the Chinese there to depend upon the goodwill of these Princes.

I believe that the tourist companies in Singapore send their clients with guides to rubber factories, rubber estates, and so forth, but an explanation of the humanity in this wonderful town and its curious customs and quaint sights would probably interest them much more ; but where to find guides with the necessary intelligence ?

OUT AND ABOUT

SINGAPORE is a town that never entirely sleeps. To it there never comes that strange lull which London and Paris know. Always there is movement in Chinatown or Campong Glam, and the wooden shoes for ever click somewhere, while work itself never entirely stops in any of the native quarters of the city.

To me there is an unending fascination in those quarters after dark has fallen and the lights are all on. A vividness and quickening seem to take place, a bustle that far out-does even that of the busy day. Such is the time when I would advise the visitor to see the town.

South-west of the river lies Chinatown, with its seething multitudes. After nightfall its theatres, coffee-shops, eating-houses, singing halls, hotels, and restaurants do a terrific business. People's Park, with its hundreds of outdoor diners and the cheap-jacks and eating-stalls along Eu Tong Seng Street, prepares you for the maze of crowded streets that thread Chinatown proper. When you have had your fill of sights here, cross over to the other side of the town and visit the New World, where you will see how the

Asiatic, and particularly the Chinese, amuses himself. Here you will find all sorts of entertaining side-shows, best of which are the Malay opera and the Chinese theatrical performances which so fascinated Charlie Chaplin when he was here. We have another amusement park called the Great World, off the River Valley Road, and it too is well worth a visit, but it is not so boisterously alive as is the New World, since it caters to a much smugger class.

To do the above properly you will need a full night and, if you go with some one who really knows the town, you will take back a vivid memory that will make the trip well worth the trouble. Any fine night will do, though naturally during Chinese New Year or the Moon festival things are at their gayest in Chinatown.

Campong Glam, as it is called, is the Malay and Arab quarter, the spine of which is North Bridge Road, with Middle Road and Arab Street as the largest ribs. Here again the best time for a visit is after dinner when the shops are a blaze of lights and the streets are full. Round Middle Road, Hailam Street, and Malay Street you will find a very gay little Japanese quarter, while around Arab Street there is much to amuse you—strange smells of flowers and food, strange things to buy or look at, great flasks of attar of roses and other perfumes, semi-precious stones, and all kinds of Oriental garments and materials.

And speaking of buying things, the most fascinating of our shops to me is that of Echigoya in Middle Road, a real Japanese shop, where you will see the most beautiful fabrics. Here you can get a proper Japanese kimono tailored to measure, and have your pick of the latest Japanese fashions which change with the seasons as do ours. Shopping in Singapore has its points, but except for the Malayan Arts and Crafts depot at Raffles Hotel, and the walking-stick shops, most of the goods you will see are foreign and better procurable in their own homes. Still, Singapore does present a bird's-eye view of Oriental arts, crafts, and fabrics that is not without merit, and a tour of the Asiatic shops in the evening before dinner will interest you.

The curio-collector in Singapore must walk like Agag. In the old days it was easy to procure at low prices very good old Chinese porcelain of the variety known to collectors as Trade, much old European silver and plate, and from time to time good pieces of jade, of Javanese and Chinese silver-work, and even old European furniture, Dutch and English. During the over-prosperous days after the war, when rubber and tin were high and people lost all sense of money values, the market was spoiled, most of the things offered being spurious ; but recently it has been returning to its old state, and good things at reasonable prices are slowly coming back. Chinese trade porcelain is particularly interesting to collect, because it comes from all sorts of quaint places and has usually been in use for generations. The Chinese during their best ceramic periods sent hundreds of junks annually to Malaysia, filled with porcelain which they traded for local produce, and the ancient records abound with advice as to the taste in different places for the different kinds of porcelain. Ancient water-bottles, rice-plates, and bowls are still procurable, some in very fine condition. Raffles Museum has a haphazard collection of trade porcelain which will give you an idea of the kind of things that still find their way here.

In Borneo, in the very old times, the Dyaks used to bury their dead in great Sung jars, to remove which is a highly dangerous undertaking. One such piece is (or was, when I was last in London) on loan in the South Kensington Museum, and I shall always remember the worried man that brought it into my office to ask my advice about it, and the tale he told me of its discovery and the difficulty he had to get it out of Borneo.

During the business hours of the day the town of Singapore is too noisy and too hot to be very attractive. Its centre of activity is in and around

Raffles Place, where are the large department stores and banks. Running out of it into Collyer Quay is a most amusing little street called Change Alley, lined on each side with cheap-jacks whose patter in very broken English will give you many a laugh, and whose extraordinary variety of goods are sold at prices that even in these hard times are astonishingly low. There are, of course, many fine buildings in Singapore, but so there are in any other large city, and they will accordingly receive from you not more than a passing glance, but the Municipal Building and the Railway Station should be entered. The latter, indeed, is unique, since it is paved and panelled with coloured rubber manufactured by the Singapore Rubber Works from a highly satisfactory patent process of their own. All noise is deadened and the artistic effect is satisfactory in the extreme, so that it is quite the most pleasing railway station you will ever visit, and it will leave you without that shattered feeling which the New York Central or Euston or the Gare du Nord inflict on one.

Museums generally are a tax on the system, unless one is of the type that haunts them wherever found, but Raffles Museum is attractive in the extreme to any one however low his or her brow may be; and no tourist in these parts should omit a visit. It is all so well arranged, so easy to see, so interesting in its contents, so cool and

RAFFLES PLACE, SINGAPORE
ONCE A MANGROVE SWAMP

THE RAILWAY STATION, SINGAPORE
BUILT ON THE SITE OF A RECLAIMED SWAMP

MOUTH OF THE ROCHORE RIVER, SINGAPORE

quiet and without that horrible dead smell that infests most of such places. Incidentally, it contains the world's finest collection of Malaysian birds and mammals, the most striking of which are publicly exhibited, while the rest are available to any one who cares to see them upon request at the Director's office.

Though the town during the day is not so pleasant, the island is delightful and there are many fine motor drives through really beautiful scenery. The coco-nut groves of Tanjong Katong and Pasir Panjang are very lovely, and there in truth on a moonlight night will you understand why a French poet once wrote so beautifully that 'the palm tree bent over the sand and offered its heart to the moon.'

Singapore possesses one little-known view that will vie with any which you will see elsewhere, no matter where you go, and that is the view from the top of Mount Faber, to which a good road will take you. Standing up there you will see spread at your feet the whole of beautiful Keppel Harbour, with clusters of distant blue islands, while on the other side you look over the whole town and docks of Singapore right out to Tanjong Katong in the east and across the island to its dim distances in the north. Unfortunately, one is not allowed to photograph or sketch these views, or I would include illustrations of them; but I do urge that from Mount

Faber you will see beauties that on no account should you miss.

There is one splendid drive round the island which I call the grand tour, and which should be taken either before breakfast when the sun is pushing away the early mists and lighting them with all the colours of mother-of-pearl, or else in the evening during the glories of the sinking sun. Let me describe it to you. Starting early in the morning before breakfast from our hotel and travelling east, we go first along Beach Road, holding our noses tight as we pass the market where the ducks and the fish emit what I am certain is the world's champion bad smell; and then we come to a very quaint little bit at the mouth of the Rochore River, round which cluster some Malay villages built on piles over the sea. They are soon to be cleared away for the new airport, so as to keep the water clear for seaplanes. All about them are native craft airing their sails after the night's dew which always falls heavily; brown, red, orange, fawn, and beige, they pick up the early light and paint a beautiful picture for us. We cross Arthur Bridge and go along the Grove Road past the site of the new airport, and turn into Fort Road, which brings us to Katong Park. If it is a fine morning, it is well worth getting out here to watch the silhouette of Singapore gradually push itself through the lavender mist, the tops of the buildings looking like some fairy town that is strangely beautiful. This is a beginning of the day that I never tire of watching from my house and that I have shown to painters, who confess it to be beyond the powers of oil and canvas, so quickly does the scene unfold and so rapidly do the colours change. Leaving the Park, we travel through Tanjong Katong and along the East Coast Road until we reach Bedoh Village with its fishing-boats, its stretches of golden sand and its beautiful view of the way to China and the East. From here we go along the winding Changi Road until we reach the Tampenis Road. If one goes on up the Changi Road one reaches a place where motor-sampans can be hired that will take one for a very pleasant trip in the Straits, and at the end of the road lies a new military cantonment which will in due course form part of the new defences of the island. This is a very beautiful part of the coast, particularly in the evening. But we turn into the Tampenis Road, with its changing vistas of scenery, and go right through it until we reach the Serangoon Road, down which we proceed until we come to the Yeo Chiu Kang Road, into which we turn and which takes us past the entrance to the Royal Air Force base and the Admiralty Wireless Station. Coming out of the Yeo Chiu Kang Road we turn to the right into the Thompson Road and travel up it as far as Seletar village, where we turn left into Mandai Road. Had we gone straight on we should have come to the great Naval Base which is now in process of construction. Mandai Road is the most beautiful in Singapore, with its long stretch of cool Forest Reserve and its soft green hills covered with pineapples. Coming out of it we turn left into Bukit Timah Road and pass the Admiralty Oil Tanks. Farther along on our left is the entrance to the Singapore Dairy Farm, which we visit and which we find surprisingly cool. The cows thrive here and seem as if they had just stepped out of a home pasturage. Though imported from Australia and the United States, they breed well and one can see the third generation doing splendidly. This Dairy Farm is a most successful and interesting experiment, highly important to the health of our white children. Returning to the Bukit Timah Road, we travel along it until we reach Reformatory Road, into which we turn, passing through it until Ayer Raja Road is reached, which we enter and then go along the road which leads over the Gap, where a fine view to sea holds us for a while. From the Gap we pass down into the Pasir Panjang Road, which takes us past Keppel Harbour, the great Empire Graving Dock, the huge Municipal Power Station, Tanjong Pagar Docks, and so into town and back to bath and breakfast at our hotel. We have then traversed between sixty and seventy miles of fine smooth roads, and have obtained the best possible idea of the island of Singapore.

That is the longest and best drive, but there are plenty of shorter ones, of which the drive round the European residential district of Tanglin and through the Botanical Gardens is a favourite one during the afternoon. The visitor will possibly be puzzled by the little boxes which he will see at the entrances to the houses and sometimes in rows at the entrances to side-roads. If he examines them he will find the name of a lady with 'not at home' under it and a slit at the top of the box into which calling cards can be placed. Frequently he will see a garden party in full blast, but, though it is perfectly obvious that the châtelaine is very heavily at home, the box outside will still inform him otherwise. There is a quaint custom in Malaya that you must never call on people when they are at home! This terribly unsocial relic dates from the days of Queen Victoria, when everybody knew everybody and the newcomer had to pay his or her respects to the whole station. As the place became bigger and bigger, it grew to be such a nuisance that a box was put out to collect the cards. The result to-day is that it is very hard indeed for the newcomer to get to know anybody.

The Bloomsbury of Singapore is the region

round River Valley Road where the huge houses of the old-time 'merchant princes,' as they loved to see themselves described, are now mostly boarding-houses. When the Settlement was first founded, the Europeans lived along the Esplanade and Beach Road; later on they moved out to the River Valley Road district; and, when I came in 1905, the top end of Orchard Road marked about the farthest point to which the European residential section reached, though some adventurous souls did live a bit farther out, notably up Orange Grove Road and Nassim Road. When the motor came, the town began to spread rapidly and it is still doing so each year; the motors killed distances, and effected as great a change here as they have done everywhere else.

Round Alexandra Road and Ayer Raja Road many ghosts must walk, for these roads formed the scene of the terrible mutiny of 1915, when over forty white people were done to death. The true story of that outbreak will probably never be written, since there are possibly not more than four or five people alive to-day who know it. I am one of them, but I learnt it all in confidence and in the course of duty, since I helped in the preliminary investigations for the Court of Inquiry and the prosecutions before the Court Martial. In any event, it is something that I wish to forget; but I would like to say that to the best of my knowledge and belief neither Mr. Diehn nor any other of our German fellow-citizens before the war had any connexion with it at all, nor is the account given in Lauterbach's book very accurate. It was engineered from India, and the channel of communication was an Indian merchant who had a house and garden near Alexandra Barracks, and who was visited continually by the native officers of the 5th Light Infantry, the Indian regiment which mutinied and which was quartered at those Barracks. A mutiny was planned to take place on February 15, 1915, in many places besides Singapore, and the 5th Light Infantry was not the only regiment which came out, though fortunately most of the other mutinies were nipped in the bud, and even in the regiment here only the Rajput wing actually mutinied; the Pathans, while doing nothing against the Rajputs, came into town and surrendered themselves and their weapons.

Along the western wall of the gaol at Pearl's Hill you will still see the bullet marks where many of the mutineers were publicly shot to death after sentence by the Court Martial; and they died like soldiers, bravely facing the firing squads and refusing to be blindfolded. The whole thing was so senseless and so wicked; these brave fellows were just cat's-paws, persuaded by lies into the doing of something that never could have affected the war in any way, and that could never have had the slightest chance of success. The Indian merchant, to whom I have referred, was tried for treason and hanged; but he again was a mere cat's-paw. It is all a bad memory, and the sooner it is forgotten the better.

But out of evil came good, for the mutiny exposed the weakness of our police arrangements and also enabled a very efficient secret service to be brought into existence. It was fortunate that we possessed at the head of the troops an officer who had been in the Intelligence during the South African War at the beginning of this century. He is to-day Major-General Sir Dudley Ridout, K.B.E., C.B., C.M.G., though at the time he was a Lieutenant-Colonel with the local rank of Brigadier-General. It was found that many spies and seditionists were coming through Singapore, but General Ridout rapidly closed down upon them and did invaluable work here with the assistance of trained officers from India; and the service which he founded is still functioning, though in changed shape, in Singapore. Just what was the condition of the Police Force in 1915 can be imagined when I tell you that the outlying police stations were not connected by telephone with the Central Police Station, so that news of the mutiny could not be telephoned in, while there was not a commissioned officer who could speak Hindustani or knew the first thing about Indians. Matters soon began to be taken in hand, and gradually there has been built up the Police Force of to-day, which is one of the prides of Singapore. The last step in its organization has been the building of big barracks and stations at central points of the town, so that the force can be properly distributed or concentrated where wanted. The largest and newest of these barracks is at the foot of Fort Canning, facing Hill Street.

The citizens and the police of Singapore are equally proud that there is very little serious crime in this city, and that a stranger can walk in any of its streets at any time of the day or night in absolute safety. In 1932 there were only twenty-one murders in the whole island, nearly all of which were followed by the discovery or conviction of the murderers.

Having thus taken you out and about, you will have realized that Singapore is quite a place. It has been made what it is to-day by the joint efforts of men of many races; and how has it been done? By free trade, by allowing any man of any race to come and trade here, by granting free access to the ships and goods of the world. This is no policy of sentiment; it is one of hard commercial common sense, and arises from the necessities of the place. A very little reflection will provide the reason. Nowadays, however, civil servants are toying with curious economic theories and we have started in a small way a policy of preference for British over foreign goods. Such a policy seems to me to be a breach of faith with the past and a denial of our fundamental faith, free trade. The Union Jack flies over us and we are part of the British Empire, but the solid fact remains that foreign races, foreign ships, and foreign goods have played as big a part in creating this great emporium as have their British counterparts, and to the lasting credit of our British merchants here they are and always have been free traders and have protested against preferential duties and the shutting out of the foreigners. There is nothing unpatriotic about this ; on the contrary, it rests upon the conviction that Britain gets a far greater benefit from a free trade Singapore than she could ever get from preferential duties here. The Buy British Campaign in Singapore was an amusing novelty while it lasted, and the highest government officials gave it their pious blessing, but what we want here is a Handle the World's Goods Campaign. That is what the place was founded for, and that is its main *raison d'être*, though another very important one, which we never used to bother about, is being forced upon our attention at this time.

It seems as if the seven angels are pouring out the vials of the wrath of God upon the earth to-day, and sitting in Singapore one is conscious of the insistent murmur of distant thunders all around one. As we have been driving about the island we have noticed much military preparation for its defence. None of it is aggressive; Britain has apparently awakened to the obvious fact that any race which might intend a hegemony over the Far East must seize Singapore first, since it is the key which opens the way to such power. As I write this, I look out over a great stretch of sheltered water where the warships of all the world could ride at anchor, and I see one of the main arteries of the world's commerce. The nation that holds such waters must protect them in the interests of world peace and must use them in the world's interest, as so far we have done by our insistence on the policy of free trade and a free port. Singapore, then, has a twofold reason for its claim to the attention of the world, as a sentinel guarding one of the main routes of the world's trade, and as an emporium standing at one of the main nodal points of that trade.

MALAYA

MALAYA is a word which you will see and hear a great deal these days, and it means that part of the Malay Peninsula which either belongs to the British or is under their protection. Actually the word has never received any official geographical imprimatur; it is a word of convenience. Foreign maps, Dutch, French, or German, call the whole Malay Peninsula by the name of Malacca. Many English people, journalists, writers, and others still frequently call the country 'Malay' or 'the Malay,' but such are ignorant persons amongst whom you obviously will not be numbered. Many people, too, in England and America think that Singapore is in India or in China. When you get back you will help to correct these quaint notions, for you at any rate will know that it is at the southernmost point of Asia, 73 nautical miles north of the Equator, and that Singapore is the name of an island containing 217 square miles (rather bigger than the Isle of Wight), and also the name of a city containing nearly half a million inhabitants, which city is the political and financial capital of Malaya.

Now actually there are seven different governments in Malaya ruling over a total population which in 1931 amounted to 4,385,346 people; and it is the painful truth that the details of these governments appear at times to be beyond the understanding of Members (and occasionally, I regret to say, even Ministers) of the English Parliament, who frequently perpetrate the most woeful solecisms. But in fact the position stands thuswise.

First of all, you have the Colony of the Straits Settlements consisting for all practical purposes of the Settlements of Singapore, Penang, and Malacca, for the fourth settlement, Labuan, in Borneo, is, alas, a mere *lapsus imperii*, a dream that went wrong. The Colony is the only part of Malaya which actually belongs to His Majesty the King-Emperor, and, despite its cosmopolitan population, it is most emphatically British, even to the point of buying British—if and when it suits.

The Settlement of Singapore includes for administrative purposes the Cocos-Keeling Islands and Christmas Island, which last is one of the most extraordinary places in the world, turning out vast quantities of phosphate of lime and containing birds and crabs that are unique.

The Settlement of Penang similarly includes for administrative purposes Province Wellesley on the mainland and the Dindings, a group of islands and a strip of mainland on the coast of Perak.

We obtained the Colony without bloodshed, and here is how it came about.

During the war with the French, which ended with the peace of 1783, the want of a good harbour in the Bay of Bengal as a resort for our ships of war had become evident. Moreover, our great trade rivals, the Dutch, were established at Malacca and had been so for more than a century. So we had to find a place which would serve as a port and as a trading station, and after other but abortive attempts the Government of India finally fixed upon the island of Penang. Francis Light, a merchant captain, was the man who brought the island to the attention of the authorities, and the East India Company purchased it from the Rajah of Kedah. The British flag was duly hoisted on August 11, 1786, and, as that day was the eve of the birthday of the First Gentleman of Europe, poor Beau Brummel's fat friend, who became George IV, the island was renamed Prince of Wales' Island and the town Georgetown. The former name has lapsed, but the latter is still the official name of the town of Penang, which last name, by the way, comes from the Malay for betel-nut (*pokok pinang*) and was given because the island abounded and still abounds with that beautiful palm.

With Malacca we played for some time a kind

of ball game with the Dutch, who had captured it from the Portuguese in 1641. The Hollanders first turned it over to us on August 12, 1795, at the written request of the last of their Stadtholders, and we occupied it as the protectors of legitimate Dutch rights which had been usurped by the Great Napoleon Bonaparte. Accordingly, on the conclusion of the Peace of Amiens in 1802 we were prepared to restore Malacca, but before we could do so war broke out again, and we continued there, fitting out in 1810 the expedition which wrested Java from the French under Marshal Daendels. In 1814 the Treaty of Vienna was signed, and under it we bound ourselves to restore Malacca and Java to the Dutch. We then looked about for a station that would command the Straits of Malacca and, owing to Stamford Raffles, picked out the island of Singapore, which the East India Company obtained from the Sultan of Johore and his chieftain the Temenggong of Singapore, from the latter of whom is descended the present Sultan of Johore. We duly occupied Singapore as from January 30, 1819, though Raffles actually landed on the island on the 28th of that month. At first we took a mere lease of part of the island, but later, on August 2, 1824, we purchased the whole island with its adjoining waters and islets to the extent of ten geographical miles.

A wonderful man, this Stamford Raffles, whose

memory is inescapable in Singapore. Munshi Abdullah, his Malay clerk, wrote of him words that I always like to remember, words which portray the perfect scholar, the perfect gentleman, and the perfect administrator. These are they: 'Now I observed his habit was always to be in deep thought. He was most courteous in his intercourse with all men. He always had a sweet expression towards European as well as native gentlemen. He was extremely affable and liberal, always commanding one's best attention. He spoke in smiles. He also was an earnest inquirer into past history, and he gave up nothing till he had probed it to the bottom. He loved most to sit in quietude, when he did nothing else but write or read; and it was his usage, when he was either studying or speaking, that he would see no one till he had finished. He had a time set apart for each duty, nor would he mingle one with another.'

'He spoke with smiles'; what better epitaph could one want?

In 1818 we restored Malacca to the Dutch, but by a treaty with them on March 17, 1824, the British and the Dutch settled all their disputes. We took the Malay Peninsula as our sphere of influence, and the Dutch took Java, Sumatra, and the rest of the Archipelago as theirs. So Malacca was handed back to us in 1825 and has remained ours ever since.

The three settlements were under the Government of India until 1867, when they were formed into a Crown Colony. We are not as yet self-governing though we do run our own cities ourselves, and when you have visited them I think you will agree that we have made a pretty good job of it.

Proceeding north from Singapore across the Causeway which joins the island with the mainland you come to the State of Johore, which belongs to His Highness Sir Ibrahim, G.C.M.G., K.B.E., &c., its Sultan, whom God protect, for he is a strong ruler, a mainstay of the Malay race, a mighty hunter and a fine figure of a man. He is a constitutional monarch, for his State has a written constitution (the only Malay State in the Peninsula which has) and his people possess a declaration from their Sultan which is in effect a Malay translation of the English Magna Carta. The State is under British protection, but is administered as a Malay State with a very small army, of which the Sultan is the Colonel Commandant, and with a civil service composed almost entirely of Malays.

Johore Bahru is the capital, and there you will find the Sultan's Palace which contains the famous Ellenborough gold plate and some interesting regalia. All tourists go to Johore, and many and wonderful are the tales which the Asiatic guides tell them, but these tales are like most out here, quite untrue. Malaya has been called the Land of Short Shadows, but the Land of Tall Stories would be just as apt.

The State of Johore is very wealthy and produces amongst other things magnificent iron-ore, said to be the finest in the world, which is mined by Japanese concessionaires who carry several hundred thousands of tons of it every year direct to Japan. Johore also is a great agricultural state, produces much rubber, and nowadays has an area of some thirty thousand acres of oil palm. It has also a large fishing industry off the east coast, and, you will be interested to learn, produces much wild rubber that is used for the manufacture of chewing-gum.

Above Johore, whose total area is about the same size as Wales (some 7500 square miles), lie the Federated Malay States, consisting of Perak, Selangor, Negri Sembilan, and Pahang. These are usually called the F.M.S. (just like that), and there are unkind cynics who say that the emphasis is on the mess. These cynics further say that the F.M.S. are always either giving away battleships or verging on bankruptcy ; but personally I loathe cynics, and I can only tell you to make a trip through these States and see when and how most of the world's rubber and tin are produced. There is a good railway with comfortable day and night accommodation, or, if you wish to motor, there are magnificent roads—none better in the world; much of the scenery is grand; there are frequent hotels and rest-houses, the whole territory is well policed, and you are safe right the way through.

British intervention in the F.M.S. caused some bloodshed, and we had military operations in Sungei Ujong, Selangor, Pahang, and Perak, but we had to do it because British subjects were being murdered and evil things were being done. The writings of those two great Malayan administrators, Sir Frank Swettenham and Sir Hugh Clifford, will describe graphically and truthfully to you the condition of affairs which brought about British intervention.

Having intervened, England chose deliberately not to annex but merely to advise through British resident officers. The present state of affairs may be said very loosely to arise from the Treaty of Pangkor in 1874, and the present federation came into existence in 1896.

Politically, the F.M.S. are under British protection, and theoretically their Sultans are absolute sovereigns; but not so that you could notice it. The hand of the Malayan Civil Service lies strong upon the land, so that in these States a person has the honour to be, and only when he has been a very, very good boy can he ever hope to be, sincerely theirs. So much, indeed, do the F.M.S. seem to be British that they have often been mentioned in the House of Commons as a British colony. However, bureaucratic domination is now apparently to be curbed and a new policy of decentralization is to be inaugurated, which seems to have upset some of the English Press Barons very much, and has caused the saying and writing of some very inaccurate things in England. The policy really is one of honesty, a return to the path which England deliberately chose when she first intervened, and I have no doubt that, if it is wisely and fairly carried out, immense good to Malaya and England will result.

Taking the States separately, Perak is much the wealthiest with its wonderful tin-mines, which can best be visited from its largest city (though, quaintly, not its capital), Ipoh. It also produces tungsten, wolfram, and a little gold, besides plenty of rubber and other agricultural produce. It comprises 7800 square miles in all, and rejoices in a very modern Sultan who is a great lover of his race, its civilization and its traditions. Kuala Kangsar, near Ipoh, is the place where the Sultan has his fine new palace, and is a very interesting and beautiful place.

Selangor (3150 square miles), though producing plenty of tin, is principally remarkable for its immense rubber acreage, and for its great colliery owned by the Malayan Collieries

Hay Wrightson, London

THEIR HIGHNESSES THE SULTAN AND SULTANAH OF JOHORE

DAWN IN THE JUNGLE, TRENGGANU

RIVER BOATS, TRENGGANU

Ltd. Its capital, Kuala Lumpur, is its largest town, being also the administrative capital of the F.M.S., and is well worth a visit. Near it are the splendid Economic Gardens, which are one of the sights of the F.M.S.; and round it there are many beautiful motor drives. The hill station called Fraser's Hill is reasonably near, and is a very pleasant place to visit in the south-west monsoon. Selangor possesses a considerable port at the mouth of the Selangor River called Port Swettenham, to which the very comfortable steamers of the Straits Steamship Company will carry you almost any day you want.

Negri Sembilan (2550 square miles) is almost entirely agricultural, but is very interesting to the student of Malay social customs as it has a peculiar exogamous, tribal, and matriarchal social organization imported from Menangkabau, the home of Malay civilization in Sumatra.

Pahang (14,000 square miles) is the most undeveloped of the States, but is the only one which produces gold in large quantities, principally from the famous Raub Gold Mine. It contains ancient gold workings that are a great puzzle and that curiously enough would seem never to have been subjected to proper archaeological exploration, a typical piece of neglect. These immense gold mines are of very ancient date and of a workmanship that has no counterpart in South-Eastern Asia. Just how interesting they are may be gathered from these words of Sir Hugh Clifford: 'Here, hidden away under the shade of the primeval forest are excavations which must have yielded in their time tons of the precious metal, and if Josephus spoke truly and did not, as is more probable, merely hazard a bold conjecture, here perhaps are to be found in the heart of the *Chersonesus Aurea* the mines of Solomon the King. Of the race that worked them, of the slaves who toiled and suffered and died therein, we to-day possess no clue, for this, the story of the earliest exploration of a portion of South-Eastern Asia, is lost to us for ever. Here, however, at the very outset of our inquiry, we obtain a glimpse of one of those pregnant suggestions wherewith Asia impresses our imaginations by virtue of her antiquity, her wonder, and her mystery. Here is the land of buried story, of hidden records, of forgotten romance.'

I quote from Sir Hugh's *Further India*, one of the most fascinating books in my library, and one that I treasure most, since it was given to me by Sir Hugh, and has a long inscription in it with much interesting personal matter. It is to me extraordinary that these ancient mines should have been left unexplored so long. The government that should long ago have undertaken this and a great deal more archaeological work, nowadays lies awake at nights thinking up schemes for retrenchment, as do most of the other governments of the world.

Pahang possesses the new hill station called Cameron Highlands, now in process of development and from which great things are expected. As I write, a new hotel is about to be opened there, and the station should prove a welcome addition to the amenities of life in Malaya and to the list of places which the tourist 'simply must visit.'

In their full prosperity the F.M.S., for their size and population, were probably the richest places in the world, and yielded to the government immense revenues, but when one totals up those revenues and contemplates the present position of the F.M.S., what they have and what they lack, there is much food for melancholy reflection. A want of public spirit on the part of the unofficial communities and too much Johnny-Head-in-Air on the part of the officials would seem to supply the reason, but nowadays a new era is dawning and the future should be brighter. The marked contrast between the Colony and the F.M.S. can, I believe, only be explained by the large part which its ordinary citizens have always played in building up the former.

As that very well-known Venetian tourist of the thirteenth century, Messer Marco Polo, was wont to observe, 'I know many more things about this country, but will now tell you about'—something else. A formula nearly as intriguing as Kipling's 'But that is another story.'

Proceeding north, we have above the F.M.S. on the west coast of the peninsula the Malay States of Kedah and Perlis, and on the east coast that of Trengganu, while between this last and Perak lies the Malay State of Kelantan. These four States are owned by their respective Sultans and have their own separate governments, but are protected by the British, the suzerainty over them having been ceded by Siam in 1906 by treaty of that year in return for financial benefits received by Siam.

Of all the Malay States, Kedah has the most ancient history, and for long has played an honourable part in the development of the civilization of the Peninsula, as you will see in a later piece called 'The Old Man of the Mountain.' Its area is 3648 square miles, and the most prominent feature in the State is Gunong Jerai, the famous Kedah Peak, opposite Penang, whose shape and beauties in the different changing lights of the day are unforgettable by all who have watched them. Rice cultivation is the principal industry, and I know of no more beautiful drive than that which takes you, mostly through ricefields, from Butterworth, opposite Penang, to Alor Star, the capital of Kedah.

Perlis is a very small Malay state next to Kedah, and contains about 316 square miles, its sole source of interest, so far as I know, being the very big limestone cave at Chuping. It has only existed as a separate State since 1841.

Trengganu has an area computed to be about 5000 square miles, but its western and inland half is mountainous and almost uninhabited. It must have great mineral potentialities, and at this date produces large quantities of iron-ore and manganese which, like that of Johore, is in Japanese hands. Much of the scenery in Trengganu is wildly beautiful, and to the explorer who wishes to tread where white men have not preceded him the State affords plenty of opportunities.

Kelantan, which has an area of 5713 square miles, is being explored to a great extent for gold, but not very much has been discovered. Its principal industry is agriculture and the raising of live stock, while in the coastal districts the Malays live mainly by fishing.

We call the five Malay States of Johore, Kedah, Perlis, Trengganu, and Kelantan by the name Unfederated Malay States, and under present conditions nothing would tempt any of them to join the federation. The preservation of Malay civilization must always be a sacred trust to its protectors, the British, and there is no race in the Empire more worthy of protection and preservation than the Malays. They are the most lovable, kindly people one could know, and far more efficient than they ever get credit for, although nowadays their value as administrators and as soldiers is being realized. If you tell a man in season and out that he is lazy and won't work, he will lose all ambition; and if you let his country be overrun by all manner of exploiters, he will deteriorate more and more and become more and more discouraged. That is very much what has happened in the F.M.S. in the past; but a new policy has now begun under which it is hoped that a better balance will be preserved between the rights of those who are developing the country and its true inhabitants. The Malays owe a debt of great gratitude to Sir Laurence Guillemard and Sir Cecil Clementi, though both of these administrators have suffered shamefully from what Renan called *la bassesse de l'homme interessé*.

I have, then, shown you that, in truly British fashion, Malaya contains no less than seven different governments, each with its own separate legislation and its own separate fiscal system; and at times a truly British muddle ensues.

Now, the Governor of the Colony is also the High Commissioner of the King for all the Malay States, federated and unfederated. As every one of these States is bound by treaty to follow his advice, which he is never in the least bashful in giving, and as he lives at Government House in Singapore, surrounded by many supermen, it is nowadays said that Singapore is the political capital of Malaya.

If you have any doubts as to its being also the financial capital, your banker will dispel them.

BRING 'EM BACK

ONE of my favourite characters in modern fiction is that very astute, very human, old American lawyer, Judge Priest, the creature of Irvin Cobb's witty brain. On a famous occasion the old Judge asked to be allowed to ramble; and I now make the same request.

We will start at a very imposing building which Government has constructed at the corner of Maxwell Road. In a room at the top of it we shall find one of the world's martyrs, Captain T. M. Hussey, Official Film Censor. During 1932 this unfortunate gentleman had to sit through no less than 4,577,700 feet of films, and not only had to censor all this but also every piece of advertising matter which accompanied it—trailers, posters, stills, and so forth. From his verdict there is an Appeal Board, but only thirty-one out of seventy-one censored films got past it in 1932. There is nothing to guide Captain Hussey but this general instruction:

'All films are objectionable which depict murders, robberies, the *modus operandi* of thieves, counterfeiters, or other criminals, violent assaults on females, or which will obviously tend to produce racial ill-feeling, set class against class, outrage the religious susceptibilities of any section of the community, bring the laws or the administration of justice into contempt or ridicule, encourage immorality, pander to salacious instincts or give rise to a feeling of unrest or insecurity.'

Enforce that rigorously in Hollywood and every lot would have its wailing wall with a long queue lined up. Also we should see precious few pictures in Singapore; so Captain Hussey and the Appeal Board endeavour to exercise a reasonable discretion: but much irritation results at times, and there is sometimes much grumbling, though my own personal view is that the censoring is extraordinarily well done. In this, as in so many other matters, we are all reduced to the lowest common denominator, the betel-nut chewer and the spitting coolie in the cheapest seats. Since there cannot be one law for one class and another for a different, Government will not allow uncensored pictures to be shown to the best class of audience in a theatre specially reserved for that class.

The cinema has made a marvellous change in Singapore life; it has, alas, driven the travelling theatrical companies off the road, but it has given us all a continuous form of amusement and often of instruction and has put plenty of money into various pockets. It has also had not a little effect on the habits, language, and costume of our populace. The snappy young Chinese salesman says 'Okay' to your requests, the Eurasian stenographer has a stab at portraying her American counterpart and parks a wad of gum while she takes dictation, and my Malay secretary once (but only once) appeared with a huge button in his coat bearing an effigy of Gloria Swanson.

Not only do we get the products of Hollywood, but London is making big inroads. Thus in 1931, 73·69 per cent. of the films imported here were American and only 5·06 British, whereas last year the latter rose to 22·01 and the former fell to 66·79, while this year the swing is still more pronounced. The balance of the remaining pictures come mainly from India or China, and a Chinese talking picture must be seen and heard to be believed, but not unless you are made of iron.

There are three first-run picture houses in Singapore and many others. Of the former the finest is the Capitol, a theatre that would do credit to any town and to fill which the management is often hard put, for Singapore audiences are extraordinarily difficult. They either like a picture or they don't; direction, technique, lighting, photography, and the finer points of acting mean nothing. The Asiatic taste makes or mars a picture, and the results are startling.

FRANK BUCK IN HIS CAMP IN JOHORE

THE ORANG UTANS

MR. BASAPA WITH APAY

Thus four gold medal pictures, *Cimarron*, *Smilin' Through*, *Strange Interlude*, and *Grand Hotel* were failures, while that magnificent picture *Farewell to Arms* flopped so hard that you could hear it in China; even *Cavalcade* has failed to make money for the exhibitors. On the other hand, *Pleasure Cruise*, an ordinary programme picture, made plenty. Comedy, music, and love interest are what the Asiatics appear to like, and anything historical leaves them cold, thus *The Rebel* had to be taken off almost at once. Of the well-known stars, Charlie Chaplin overtops them all, while Maurice Chevalier, George Arliss, Norma Shearer, Janet Gaynor, Jeannette Macdonald, Marie Dressler, and Ronald Colman are sure-fire; but Sylvia Sidney, Joe E. Brown, Marlene Dietrich, and even Greta Garbo mean nothing here. George Raft and Mae West are unknown, since they have been censored out of existence so far; Jean Harlow's pictures have been so badly cut by the Censor that Singapore hardly realizes her capabilities. Wheeler and Woolsey are by far the greatest favourites as a comedy team, while Laurel and Hardy and the Marx Brothers seem to be beyond the natives though great favourites with the children. The Wheeler and Woolsey popularity reached its zenith when they were shown a year or two ago in a special trailer, where they spoke Malay to the audience, and their recent personal visit clinched their position. These personal visits do the stars much good; we have seen Charlie and Syd Chaplin here, Will Rogers and Richard Barthelmess, and Singapore liked them all. Mr. Joe Fisher, the doyen of our exhibitors, vouches the accuracy of the information in this paragraph.

Mickey Mouse is a roaring success, and one of the most pleasant things one can do here is to drop in at a matinée of the Mickey Mouse Club at the Capitol, which is packed with a mass of children of all races who roar their approval and applause in a most stimulating way. Sometimes the members do a bit of entertaining themselves, and the other day I saw a small Chinese boy, about knee high to a grass-hopper, march on to the stage and perform an intricate piano solo in a way that surprised even me, accustomed as I am to surprises in this strange city.

Mr. Joe Fisher tells me that the greatest financial successes in Singapore so far have been *Love Parade*, *Sunnyside Up*, *Tarzan*, *East of Borneo*, and *Samarang*, while naturally *Bring 'em Back Alive* rang the bell; and that takes me rambling off to Johore where Frank Buck has his camp as I write this, for he is making a new animal picture to be called *Wild Cargo*. He has been collecting wild animals so long down here and is so well known that Singapore counts him as an honorary citizen, so that one is glad that it was he who put Singapore so emphatically on the movie map with *Bring 'em Back Alive*, and set an example which during the past year has been followed by many others. He has had the most remarkable adventures, as his books tell you, and has had several close calls from death. The animals which you see in his pictures are really wild ones, as savage as can be, and to see Frank Buck handle them gives a thrill that no animal trader can rival. Making the necessary allowances for the necessities of the camera, Buck's pictures are the real thing; but don't imagine that Singapore itself is full of wild animals and snakes, for it is not. You can live on this island for a quarter of a century and see none besides the monkeys in the Botanical Gardens, the animal shops, and the Singapore Zoo; which is now one of the sights of the town.

The Singapore animal trade was started in 1880 by a Malay named Haji Marip, who carried on the business until his death in 1915. Many followed his example, and in Rochore Road to-day there are several Chinese dealers, but our two best-known collectors are Mr. Herbert de Souza, who has his collection at the East Coast Road, and Mr. W. L. S. Basapa, the proprietor of the Singapore Zoo at Ponggol, a truly delightful place that has the full approval of the local animal authorities. Here you will see a magnificent collection of birds, amongst which the crown pigeons are said to be the best in the world. The *orang utans* are really happy here and in a climate natural to them. They are playful little fellows and perfectly safe to handle, the friends of all the Singapore children who go to the Zoo. There is also a great tiger named Apay who came to the Zoo as a baby, and who, though he is now four years old, can still be led on a chain. If you go alone to his cage and talk gently to him he will roll on his back and purr like a cat. He has been used in several pictures made here recently, as have others of Mr. Basapa's animals, particularly the *orang utans*, which are great favourites. By the way, *orang utan* is Malay for man of the jungle and should not be spelled *orang outang* as it so often is. Mr. Basapa tells me that climatic conditions in Singapore are such that one of the best Zoos in the world could be kept here; and it seems a great pity that his place is not taken over permanently and made into a really fine public show. We are just about to embark on an Aquarium which will be publicly owned, and one hopes that one day there will also be a really big Zoo and a local Zoological Society. As it is, I think that the town owes much to Mr. Basapa's very courageous lone effort in providing us with what is really a great attraction; and I hope that he is receiving all the support which he is entitled to expect. A trip to the Zoo is one of the things that no visitor should omit; it has a personality entirely its own, and is pitched in beautiful surroundings on the Straits of Johore.

If Frank Buck brings 'em back alive, the Sultan of Johore and Mr. Theodore Hubback bring 'em back dead, for they are the mightiest hunters who have ever been in Malaya; indeed, Frank Buck says that His Highness is the greatest Asiatic big-game hunter in the world, and any time in the wilder parts of Johore one is liable to hear the roar of his great Mercedes. Some man-killing tiger has been located and His Highness is out to save his villagers. He does not hunt his tigers from a fortress on the top of an elephant or sitting up in a tree; he fetches them on foot, and only takes a bearer or two and perhaps a friend with him.

And now let me ramble off to distant Pahang and introduce you to Mr. Theodore Hubback, the Game Warden for Malaya, and one of the world's authorities on wild life preservation, whose recent report is already a classic on the subject. He, like the Sultan of Johore and Frank Buck, is a man whom, having once seen, you will always remember; and he possesses a pair of the most unforgettable blue eyes I have ever seen, the true eyes of a hunter and a lover of the open.

Myself, I possess a defect of the eye which makes it almost impossible to hit anything at which I aim, and I am a total loss anywhere except in a city; but as I enjoy the friendship of Theodore Hubback, and as he is the most long-suffering of men, he has provided me with some splendid photographs which I reproduce, and with the notes from which I am able to tell you about the big game of the Peninsula and how and where it can be shot.

The Malay Peninsula has been greatly endowed with a beautiful and varied fauna, but save in the remoter parts it is almost impossible to reach. Malaya is the habitat of two species of rhinoceros, elephant, two species of wild cattle, tiger leopard and clouded leopard, the magnificent sambar deer, and hundreds of species of birds, amongst which can be found the resplendent argus pheasant; and it might well have been proud of such natural possessions, but the rapid opening up of the country and the pursuit of wealth, combined with an almost total lack of interest on the part of past governments, has squandered them. It is seldom realized until too late that wild life, especially such a variety of large and small game as could be found in Malaya, is a source of wealth and an attraction to a country, and now that most of the large game animals are so rapidly disappearing from Malaya there is much fuss but little determination to save what is left. The Press and the public are expecting Mr. Hubback's recommendations to

THEODORE HUBBACK WITH SOME TROPHIES

THEODORE HUBBACK AT THE END OF A LONG TRAIL

MALAYAN SELADANG

MALAYAN ELEPHANT

be carried out, and we hope that Government will create a National Game Park for Malaya, which would be a great addition to the country's attractions and a valuable asset. The proposal was first put forward in April 1927, so that it ought to have had time to sink in by now!

Such steps as have been taken to preserve and protect wild life in Malaya so far have been deplorably defective and without any co-ordination; what has been everybody's business has been nobody's business.[1] But there is still a little large game left, and it may be interesting to you to know where such game is to be found and how it can be killed; and here a curious paradox enters. The worst thing that can befall any species of game is for it to reach the stage where it has to be entirely protected from legitimate hunting. The best friends of conservation of wild life have always been and always will be those whose knowledge has been founded upon the following and observation of species for the purpose of sport. The hunter learns more about his quarry than any stay-at-home theorist can ever hope to know, and knowledge so gleaned almost invariably leads to a desire to see that wild life should be treated fairly and, in the case of animals or birds which are considered as coming within the realms of

[1] Since writing the above, the State of Johore has set a splendid lead by creating a large Wild Life Sanctuary.

sport, that their pursuit should be governed by strict rules and regulations.

To all persons the destruction of the immature of such animals as elephants, wild cattle, deer, and other large mammals must be abhorrent, yet such acts take place frequently in Malaya under the present regulations.

The legitimate hunting of large game when the quarry consists of old and mature bulls is not only a thrilling and arduous form of recreation, but is also an act which can in no way harm the species, because very frequently the oldest bulls (which carry the finest trophies) are no longer either desired by or useful to the herds from which they so frequently absent themselves. An old elephant or an old seladang (species of wild cattle) has no peaceful passing away; old age brings a miserable death from semi-starvation or from a tiger. The kindest and most merciful death is the sportsman's bullet.

Although conservation of wild life, as practised in more enlightened countries, has not yet reached Malaya, there is, as I said, legitimate sport still to be found if you know where to look for it and how to organize your expedition.

On the west coast of the Peninsula big game hunting has practically passed away, but on the east coast, in Pahang, Trengganu, and Kelantan, good big game hunting and at certain seasons of the year good river fishing can be obtained.

The pursuit of elephant and seladang affords magnificent sport, and the trophies obtainable will well repay an enthusiastic hunter for any trouble to which he may go. Seladang, however, are very dangerous animals.

Licences have, of course, to be obtained, and they cost for non-residents from $80 (Straits) for one head to $200 for four head. The use of a small-bore high velocity rifle is not encouraged in the dense Malayan jungles. The Chief Game Warden will always give full information and assistance to any one who wishes to obtain sport in Malaya; and the local Game Wardens will, no doubt, help in making the arrangements for an expedition, if sufficient notice is given.

If photography of big game is desired, trips can be made to the game reserves where it would be possible to see and probably photograph the magnificent Malayan wild cattle called seladang. Shooting, naturally, is not allowed in these reserves, but the country where game can be hunted is not far from them, so that sport and photography can be combined.

I have said that a small-bore high velocity rifle is not encouraged, and Mr. Hubback utters a strong word of warning. He says that a heavy rifle is absolutely necessary for use when going after big game in Malaya. All one's shooting is taken at short range, nearly always within twenty-five yards, and frequently at a much shorter distance than that, and in thick jungle. Accurate aim at some well-defined vital spot is seldom possible. Any rifle less than a ·450 bore cordite, or a super-cordite rifle, firing not less than 55 grains of nitro powder, should not be used. Double-barrelled rifles are always recommended for the close shooting invariably obtained in the dense cover where big game is likely to be found.

Few of the present generation of Malays are any use as trackers. Many will pretend that they are, in order to get your favour and your money, but unless recommended by an experienced European sportsman, they should be avoided. By far the best trackers in Pahang, which is where you are likely to go for your sport, are Sakai, the aboriginal tribes, which, speaking generally, frequent the mountainous country.

Sakai are natural trackers; all their lives they have lived in primeval jungle and, from childhood to old age, they notice everything just ahead of them when walking along the jungle paths. There is instilled into them, accordingly, an uncanny gift of being able to follow the trail of an animal through the jungle without any fuss or bother: a disturbance of the leaves, a broken spider's web, a break in the earth are sign-posts to them. As a race they are expert trappers but not expert hunters, so that their knowledge of these matters has not come to them because of the toilsome following of tracks with the object of killing something, but because all their lives they have had to watch their step. Snakes, centipedes, scorpions, and sharp snags are unpleasant things on which to place a naked foot.

Sakai will track, carry heavy loads, help to make your camp, eat as much as they can get hold of, from frogs and lizards to large game—some tribes, however, will not eat elephant—but are little good when trophies are being prepared; that you must do yourself. I have been told that when Cameron Highlands was first opened up not a sound could be heard nor a living thing seen; insects, birds, mammals, the Sakai had eaten everything. They must lead a terribly hard life, and were driven into the mountains ages ago by the more civilized plainsmen. Even in quite recent times the old Sultans of Pahang used to organize an annual Sakai hunt, of one of which Sir Hugh Clifford has written a very graphic description.

The quarry that any big game hunter coming to Malaya would almost certainly wish to secure would be the seladang, or Malayan gaur, the largest species of wild cattle found in the world to-day, and a very dangerous animal to the careless. The mature and ageing bulls will stand eighteen hands at the shoulder and will weigh over 2000 pounds. A well-mounted head is one of the finest trophies a hunter's heart can desire, and is well worth any hardship which he may have to endure. All hunting is carried on by tracking. The fresh tracks of what one wishes to obtain must be found, and then the trail is followed until the animal is met. Nineteen times out of twenty, especially when hunting seladang or rhinoceros, nothing will eventuate; either the animal will not be seen that day or, if met, will become aware of the hunter and decamp before it is seen. Mr. Hubback tells me he has followed rhinoceros very frequently and has obtained one or two trophies, but invariably the hunting is long and arduous, and only by much persistence can these animals be bagged. One old rhinoceros, wise even beyond his years, was followed by Mr. Hubback for thirty-one days during three occasions and was only heard twice but never seen at all. So it must not be imagined that big game hunting in Malaya is either easy or simple; it is very much the reverse, but for the real fellow it is the class of hunting which he will desire.

Tiger hunting in Malaya is a casual sport which is only happened on and for which no arrangements can be made (except in a few localities) for tying up for a kill. A hunter would be able to ascertain when on his trip

TO-MORROW WILL BE FRIDAY

if there was any news of tiger in his locality. Tiger beating is impossible in this country and is never attempted as a sport.

In Johore, however, there are plenty of tiger, and in 1932 no less than forty-five persons were killed by them. Up the rivers in Johore, also, there is good crocodile shooting to be had.

Mr. Hubback tells me that there is some very fine fishing to be had in the beautiful rivers up-country, but one has to go far from the haunts of man to find it, owing to an entire lack of fish conservation. There is a fish in the upper reaches of our larger rivers which very much resembles the mahseer of India, and which is known as *tengas*, while the *sebarau*, a fine fighting fish, is the best known of Malayan sporting fish; and there are several other varieties that will give the angler all the thrills he wants.

Even if you do not wish to kill, a trip into the Malayan wilds is a fine thing for the healthy and fit. In the hunting and fishing country the up-river scenery is superb, and, entirely apart from the enjoyment of the sport that can be obtained, the stay in untrodden parts, the great trees and magnificent scenery, the clear crystal streams, the call of the argus pheasant, the smell of the camp fire, the lazy evenings free from mosquitoes—for they are seldom found in unopened jungle—will combine in providing the peace and mental rest of a real holiday, far away from the chattering noisy life which now passes as civilization. It is surprising how few residents, much less visitors, ever avail themselves of the opportunity to be alone with this beautiful aspect of nature. Here is a trip which the tourist agencies might well organize and exploit.

And now I have finished my ramble, and I am quite sure that you will find Mr. Hubback's by far its most interesting part. He loves his jungle and its creatures; he lives more or less in it; and I am quite sure that his knowledge and assistance would always be at the disposal of any true sportsman.

ANCIENT MARINERS

TAKE your map of Asia, and there in the middle between west and east lies India, with the Arabian Sea, the Persian Gulf, and the Red Sea on its west, the Bay of Bengal and the Straits of Malacca on its east, and the Indian Ocean on its south.

The monsoons blow up from the south-west for part of the year and down from the north-east for the other part. The Malay Peninsula lies between India and China, the south-west and north-east monsoons bringing sailing craft up and down each side of it. At the nodal point lies Singapore, with a safe anchorage, easily navigable straits, and in the old days covered with fine straight timber especially suitable for masts and spars.

Taking the effect of the monsoons we see that sailing ships from China, Indo-China, and Siam would come down on the north-east monsoon and go back on the south-west, while those from India left their ports on the south-west and returned on the north-east. Such ships as wanted to continue their journey up the Straits of Malacca to India or in the opposite direction up to China, would wait for the change of monsoon at some port which would naturally be either on the sheltered coasts of the Malay Peninsula or of Sumatra or else at the foot of the Peninsula.

To such a port would also come the produce of the Malayan Archipelago, and it is obvious that collecting and transhipment stations for cargo would be necessitated, because the majority of the ships from India or China would find it more economical to come down, exchange their cargoes for fresh ones, and then go back rather than make the trip right round.

Geography, economics, and the winds, therefore, brought into existence entrepôts and commercial emporiums; and such places must have existed in or near the Straits of Malacca from the time when sea trade first began between India, the Malay Archipelago, and China. We shall see in later pieces that the most important of these in historic times were at or near the place in Sumatra which is now called Palembang, at Singapore, and later at Malacca.

What human beings exactly formed the Malay race physically and what civilization first came into the Malay Peninsula and Archipelago are matters of dispute. It does, however, seem clear that the Malays are part of that widespread race which ethnologists call the Malayo-Polynesians, whose powers of migration by sea were so startling that they are found from Madagascar in the west to Easter Island in the east, and from Formosa in the north to New Zealand in the south. Basically they appear to be Mongoloids.

A stone-age culture spreading through Burma, Siam, Indo-China, and the Malay Peninsula has been discovered, which the great authority on Indian archaeology, Sir J. H. Marshall, thinks was produced not by the aboriginal tribes but by later invaders who were in a more advanced state of civilization. Of those aboriginal inhabitants there seem to have been two main streams, negritoes or Semangs, and the peoples whom we call Sakai, both of whom are still to be found in the Malay Peninsula. The stone-age culture of Malaya will be found well illustrated in Raffles Museum, where there is a stone axe-head found on Singapore Island and made from local stone.

It would seem that long before the curtain of history can be lifted on Malaysia, some ancient civilization, traces of which are found almost all over the world, had penetrated into the Malay Archipelago and thence into Polynesia, as is evidenced by the terraced agriculture, the stone buildings and pyramids, the megaliths, the mummification and the worship of the sun and the sky, that are to be found scattered through the Archipelago and Polynesia. There would also seem to be much evidence of this in the folklore of these places. Raffles, in his *History of Java*, 1817, mentions the then current tradition that Java was civilized by banishees from ancient Egypt.

In Sumatra, too, there is some evidence to be found in a series of rudely sculptured images which are very reminiscent of the extraordinary, and as yet unexplained, giants of Easter Island, and there are still legends extant there of a mystic civilization which preceded that introduced from India.

Insufficient investigation makes it impossible to say at present whether there are any traces of this ancient civilization in the Malay Peninsula. A very curious megalith has, however, been discovered in Negri Sembilan. There are also remains of ancient gold mines, gigantic workings, abandoned no man knows how long, and unfortunately still not investigated. Such remains occur, amongst other places, at Mount Ophir near Malacca, at Belum in Upper Perak, and particularly at Selinsing in Pahang. Round many of such old workings stone implements have been found. One can only hope that some day systematic research will be made into all the old mine workings in the Peninsula, for one feels sure that valuable data will result.

From one thousand years before the birth of Christ, we can begin to draw an accurate picture of the ancient Indian trade, as it is called, the backbone and richest part of which came from Malaysia.

In the west we find King Solomon (about 1015 B.C.) picking up the sea-borne trade from India and growing fabulously rich, for those times, upon its proceeds, and we find Phoenician seamen handling that trade up the Red Sea and across the Mediterranean. Many writers have identified, and still identify, the Malay Peninsula with Solomon's Ophir. It is also definitely asserted by many that Phoenician seamen made voyages all along the coasts of the Indian Ocean, penetrated the Straits of Malacca, and passed on into the Chinese seas, and it is said that they were the carriers of that ancient civilization, of which I have already spoken, into the Malay Archipelago. Others again assert that ancient Egyptians brought it.

Whatever be the case, people to-day are too apt to forget that, though in its wrath the sea is a thing of mighty terror, nevertheless it has been man's best friend; over it he could move in ancient times more swiftly and more easily than he could over the land, by its use he was able to discover and civilize, to teach and to learn, more than in any other way. Accustomed to travelling in ships of large burthen, we are too apt to underrate the sailing capacities of man, but Drake, Columbus, and Vasco da Gama, did they live to-day, could tell us what can be done in safety with a thirty-ton sailing ship or less.

Certain it is that innumerable centuries ago trade and the search for necessary commodities sent men on long sea voyages, for we find that a thousand years before the birth of Christ sea commerce was fully organized in the Mediterranean, the Red Sea, and the Indian Ocean. Thus, early Chaldaean inscriptions speak of the ships of Ur, its capital; and there is clear evidence that from at least the fourteenth century before Christ, gold, silks, spices, pearls, &c., had been passing from India to the Assyrian monarchy, carried both by land and by the coasting trade by sea. The ancient Indian literature known as the *Rig-Veda*, which the best authorities date as from 1000–800 B.C., has references to 'merchants under the influence of greed sending out ships to foreign countries,' and again to 'merchants whose field of activity knows no bounds, who go everywhere in pursuit of gain, and frequent every part of the sea.'

Just as mosquitoes carry malaria, dengue, and yellow fever, so do seamen and merchants carry cultures round the world, which explains in part the similarity of many ancient things and many religious beliefs which you will notice on your travels. The most obvious instance for a traveller to Singapore is that of the eyes on Chinese boats. There is the good old explanation in pidgin English, 'No got eye, no can see—what fashion can go?' The real fact, however, is that you will find these eyes on all sorts of boats everywhere, in out-of-the-way parts of the world, in India, China, Malaysia, the Pacific region, North America, British Columbia, Ceylon, all round the Mediterranean and, as I said before, almost everywhere. The very earliest known representations of ships show eyes on them; and the origin of the custom is quite clearly to be found in the protecting eye of Horus, one of the oldest gods of the ancient Egyptians, who painted it on their boats as a protective talisman. Incidentally, the single lock of hair which small Malay boys wear can be traced back to the lock of Horus; but we won't go into that.

So for more than one thousand years before Christ, thoughts, beliefs, customs, and language have been carried back and forth through the world; and Malaysia presents to the inquirer a marvellous cat's cradle of them which is slowly being unraveled.

But to return from these digressions, the earliest records of India are contemporaneous with the Bible, and, giving thereafter a continuous picture, they show that for thirty centuries India was one of the foremost maritime countries of the Old World, with colonies in Burma, Indo-China, and Malaysia. She was the first historic civilizer of the Malay Peninsula, and her leading seamen of ancient times were the Tamils of southern India, as to which I write in the next essay.

Long before the Christian era these Tamils were carrying on a thriving trade with Western Asia, Egypt, and later with the Greek and Roman Empires. Their influence on Western nations can be found in the Tamil that passed into the Hebrew of the Bible and from the Greek language into our own. Thus pepper, rice, ginger, and cinnamon, to take four very well-known commodities, are all Tamil words, respectively, pippali, ariçi, injiver, and karppu, and reached English through the Greek versions of those words.

At first it was the Tamil seamen who fetched the goods of China and passed them through other seamen in the Red Sea into Europe, but later the Chinese themselves began to find their way south. Cautiously and by degrees they worked their way down to Cambodia, round the Gulf of Siam, down the east coast of the Malay Peninsula, up the Straits of Malacca, and to Ceylon and India. In their records you can watch them doing this.

In the early centuries of the Christian era, then, we have Indian and Chinese seamen passing Singapore on their lawful occasions; and we must now turn to Europe in the west.

Just as one reads that Columbus discovered America and Harvey discovered the circulation of the blood, so one reads that a Greek sea-captain named Hippalus discovered and was the first to make use of the monsoons in about A.D. 47; but, in reality, all that is true in each of the three cases is that they were the first Europeans to do so. In short, they merely rediscovered; and it is perfectly certain that the Indians and Persians knew all about the monsoons long before Hippalus.

With the discovery of the Greek captain, Western geography begins almost at once. In about A.D. 60 an anonymous Greek merchant-captain wrote a kind of guide-book called the *Periplus* of the Erythraean Sea (that is, Voyage around the Indian Ocean) and in it he also tells, but from hearsay and vaguely, what was known of the way to China. Then in A.D. 77 Pliny, a Roman admiral, published his Natural History, which pushes definite knowledge as far as Ceylon; and about A.D. 150 Ptolemy, a Greek born in Alexandria, published his famous Geography, and knowledge now reaches the Malay Peninsula, called Chryse or the Golden Chersonese, but Ptolemy's knowledge of this and China beyond is still inaccurate and very short of detail. It is an interesting fact that in these three works is to be found the largest stock of Dravidian words contained in any written documents of ancient times; and the Dravidian languages are, broadly speaking, those of southern India, the most cultivated of them being Tamil.

Greek sailors or Yavanas, as the Tamils called them from Iaones, their own name for themselves, began to push into India and beyond, through the Straits of Malacca, past Singapore to China. We find Yavana soldiers in the employ of Tamil kings, and Yavana wines and other commodities in great demand among the Tamils, while the early Chinese records tell of Yavanas in China. These Greeks were, of course, Roman subjects. In 1927 there was found in a remote corner of lower Siam (at a place near the ancient land route across the Peninsula from lower Burma along the Kanburi River into Siam) a Graeco-Roman oil lamp made of bronze exactly similar to those which the ruins of Pompeii and Herculaneum have yielded by hundreds. I know of no more interesting antiquity in South-Eastern Asia than this mute witness to the extent of ancient trade; it is to be seen in the Bangkok Museum.

At the beginning of the Christian era and in the reign of Augustus (to whom, incidentally, there was a temple in one of the principal Tamil ports) the Indian trade with Rome reached its height and sowed the seeds of the decline of that Empire. Luxury grew more and more rife in

Rome, reaching its culmination in Nero's time (A.D. 54–68), and the women in particular clamoured for Malaysian tortoiseshell, spices, and perfumed woods, for Indian muslins, Chinese silks, and other costly Eastern luxuries which Pliny says sold in his time at prices representing one hundred times their cost. Economists and moralists raged; the former because, the trade being almost entirely adverse, over a million of our pounds' worth of Roman gold went to India year after year and the gold balance was upset; the latter because society deteriorated by luxury, and the women, wearing more and more transparent Indian muslins, made their bodies more sensual and caused sexual vice to abound.

Curiously enough, the same kind of thing happened in China during the Sung Dynasty, when the trade of China with India and Malaysia reached its greatest extension in the eleventh and twelfth centuries of our era. This trade was principally one way, into China, so that there was a tremendous drainage of Chinese coinage, and not only were the Chinese affected economically but also morally, as had been the Romans, and stern sumptuary laws were passed by them also, but the evils continued uncheckable until the Mongols became the rulers of China.

Finally, from the ninth century of our era,

and probably long before, there was a flow of Arab and Persian seamen into Malaya and beyond into China. Upon the trade of India and Malaysia the Arab power and that of the Caliphs of Bagdad was built, and Arab records abound with curious information about the trade and customs of Malaysia. The Arabs eventually introduced Islam into Malaysia, so that to-day almost all its indigenous inhabitants are Mohammedans.

After the Arabs and Persians came the 'red-faced barbarians,' as the Chinese called them—that is, the Portuguese, Dutch, and British.

So you see that the waters which ebb and flow past Singapore tell the history of the world, and to me there are none more romantic anywhere. I for one never look out upon them without thinking of all the brave seamen who have sailed them.

And how did these sailors navigate, and what like were their ships?

Buddhism was an international religion and encouraged intercourse with foreign nations, so that the early Buddhist literature in particular abounds in references to sea voyages. It tells us that the Indian ships of the sixth century before Christ were large enough to hold seven hundred people, and there are many allusions to ships carrying three, five, and seven hundred people. We know, however, that the ancient ships of all times were grossly overcrowded.

The *Periplus* tells us that the Indian ships were vessels of great bulk and adapted to the voyages made to the Golden Chersonese, while Chinese records of the eighth century say that the Indian ships which visited Canton were very large, and so high out of the water that ladders several tens of feet in length had to be used to get aboard. The captains had to register with the Inspector of Maritime Trade, to whom they had to submit their manifests and who collected duties and freight charges through his office. In the twelfth century A.D. the ships are described as like houses; 'When their sails are spread they are like great clouds in the sky.' A single ship carried several hundred men and a year's supply of grain besides live stock, and liquors which they fermented on the voyage. As far back as the seventh century the Indian ships were described by the Chinese as being two hundred feet long and carrying from six to seven hundred men. They had large barques or tenders attached to them, and used long sweeps as well as sails.

We hear of Chinese ships in the fifteenth century of 440 feet in length and 180 feet in beam, but this sounds like an exaggeration. We do, however, know that in the early part of the nineteenth century Chinese junks of as much as 1200 tons burthen used to come down from China, and we are told that except before the wind they were very unwieldy, requiring at times as many as fifty men to manage the helm. Such ships took from twenty to twenty-five days to make the voyage from Amoy to Batavia. The average time for a junk to Singapore was about eighteen to twenty days. The voyage to the Southern Seas, as the Chinese called Malaysia, has always followed from the earliest times a course in sight of land as far as Condore Island, after which the junks put boldly out to sea on the north-east monsoon, aiming for Tioman Island off the east coast of the Malay Peninsula, whence they would head for Bintang Hill, which served as a finger-post guiding the junks for Singapore into the Strait and those for Java southward past the islands round Bintang.

From the sixth to the twelfth centuries A.D. the captains trusted, when out of sight of land, to the regularity of the monsoons and steered solely by the sun, moon, and stars, taking soundings as often as possible. It was also customary to keep pigeons on board by which they used to send messages to land. These captains had a curious method of ascertaining their position, which they did by means of long lines to which were attached a heavy fluke. When this fluke was hauled in, they determined their whereabouts by the smell of the mud brought up. The Buddhist bonzes summed up the whole position by saying, 'To cross the sea is dangerous, but pray and you will see to the vault of heaven, and in nothing will help fail you.'

The compass, or 'south-pointing needle,' as the ancient Chinese called it, is first mentioned in the twelfth century A.D., but the Indians long prior thereto had used nautical instruments, principally the astrolabe or armillary sphere. A monument found on Karimon Island records the possession of one of the latter in about the eighth century A.D.

The earliest record of a voyage from India to Malaysian waters is that of a Chinese monk named Fa-Hsien, who sailed in the fifth century A.D. He encountered a terrible storm which raged for thirteen days and nights, and of this he has left a vivid description. He says of his voyage that the sea was infested with pirates, to meet whom was death. 'The expanse of ocean is boundless, east and west are not distinguishable; only by observation of the sun, moon, and constellations, is progress to be made. In cloudy and rainy weather, our vessel drifted at the mercy of the wind, without keeping any definite course. In the darkness of night nothing was to be seen but the great waves beating upon one another and flashing forth light like fire, huge turtles, sea-lizards, and such-like monsters of the deep. Then the merchants lost heart, not knowing whither they were going, and the sea being deep, without bottom, they had no place where they could cast their stone anchor and stop. When the sky had cleared, they were able to tell east from west, and again to proceed on their proper course; but had they struck a hidden rock, there would have been no way of escape.' The sailors attributed their ill-luck to the priest's presence, and considered throwing him overboard. So Fa-Hsien would seem to be the earliest instance of the sailors' belief that a clergyman on board a ship means bad luck.

Our old friend the sea-serpent turns up in a Chinese book of the twelfth century A.D., which gives a good recipe for dealing with him. 'When the ship is in mid-ocean, if suddenly there is seen in the distance something like a clump of islands covered with dried trees and the captain has reason to believe that there is no land in that place, they know that it is the sea-serpent. Then they cut off their hair, take fish scales and bones and burn them, upon which it will gradually disappear in the water.'

The whale was known under the name of dragon, and ambergris was called dragon's spittle, there being an island off the west of Sumatra where great quantities of it used to collect, so that the island was known as Dragon-Spittle Island.

It was not until the beginning of the sixteenth century that the 'red-faced barbarians' entered the Straits of Malacca. First came the Portuguese, then the Dutch and English. The Portuguese expeditions were outfitted by their king, and the vessels were very large for the times, being from 1500 to 1600 tons burthen, and carrying crew and soldiers to the number of five to six hundred. The first English expeditions were purely trading ventures by joint-stock speculators, who consisted, it was quaintly said, 'of dukes and earls, knights, judges, the King's council, privy-counsellors, countesses and ladies, doctors of divinity and physic, widows and virgins'; which shows that in some respects the times have not changed very much. The early English ships were very small compared to the others I have mentioned.

The Portuguese and Spaniards divided the world between them under the Pope's famous Bull of 1493, by which the former got the eastern part as a result of their rounding of the Cape of Good Hope in 1487, and the latter got the western part as a result of the discovery of America by Christopher Columbus in 1492. It must be remembered that Columbus sailed west in search of the Indies and their rich trade; and to his dying day he believed that America was the western edge of Asia, a belief preserved to-day in the name of West Indies. The Spaniards, again in the search for the Indies towards the west, crossed South America and also rounded Cape Horn. They reached the Spice Islands in due course, but, making no headway, concentrated on the Philippine Islands.

And there we will leave our ancient mariners, paying a tribute to their memory and marvelling at the courage and fortitude which they displayed.

THE OLD MAN OF THE MOUNTAIN

FROM Singapore it is easy to reach Indo-China, Siam, Java, and Bali. Wherever you travel in these places you are liable to be reminded of India, its religions, its customs, and its art, the reason for which is that South Indians were the first civilizers in historic times of South-Eastern Asia. Amongst the world's most wonderful ruins are those of Angkor in Indo-China, and of the Borobodur and the other temples on the plain of Prambanan in Java, while amongst the world's most picturesque peoples are the inhabitants of Bali. These famous places can convey but a fraction of their message unless one is acquainted with the great story that lies behind them.

Just as you notice the prevalence of our Western civilization in all the main places which you visit in South-Eastern Asia to-day, so the traveller would have noticed the South Indian civilization prevalent during the earliest centuries of the Christian era; and to explain this we must go back to the South Indian seamen and merchants of whom I spoke in the preceding essay.

The principal South Indian kingdoms with which we are concerned were those of the Kalingas, Pallavas, and Cholas. The territory of the first lay along the north-eastern coast of India, their capital being where the present town of Calingapatam is situated, and their principal port at Masulipatam; below them on the Coromandel coast lay the country where first the Pallavas and then the Cholas had the seats of their kingdoms.

The Kalinga kingdom appears some centuries before Christ, and in various forms and with very varying fortunes Kalinga kings continue to appear until the fourteenth century A.D. It was due to the terrible carnage which attended the sacking of Kalinga in 262 B.C. that the great Emperor Asoka turned to Buddhism, which in due course became the State relation of South India and remained so until the fifth century A.D., when it was supplanted by Brahmanism. From inscriptions it is known that navigation and ship commerce formed part of the education of Kalinga princes; and Indian tradition says that it was a Kalinga prince who first brought South Indian civilization into Java and established the Saka era, which still prevails there and which dates there from A.D. 75. To this day all Tamils from the eastern coast of India are called in Malay *orang Kling*, that is Kling men or men of Kalinga, and the Malay Annals contain many references to Kling rajahs. The Kling of to-day is mostly a lowly person who does coolie work on the roads and the rubber plantations, so that the better class of South Indians object to being called Klings, and we have had to change the name of one of Singapore's oldest streets from Kling Street to Chulia Street, but in the name lies a reminder of the most glorious days of South India. Chulia, it may be noticed, is merely the Northern Indian name for the same people as the Malays call Klings.

In the first centuries of our era there appeared in South-Eastern Asia a number of South Indian kingdoms, of which the most important were the Mon or Talaing kingdom at Pegu in Lower Burma; the kingdom in Indo-China which the ancient Chinese called Fou-Nan, and from which the great Khmer empire arose, with its capital at Angkor in Cambodia; the Cham kingdom of Champa in what is now Cochin-China; and the Sumatran kingdom of Sri-Vijaya, with its capital at or near the spot where Palembang stands to-day.

It is with this last that the ancient history of the Malay Peninsula is most concerned, and it is to its monarch that I have disrespectfully referred in the title of this essay. Actually he was known as the Maharajah, King of the Mountain and Lord of the Isles, his family being known as that of Sailendra. He is the Maharajah who appears in the voyages of Sindbad, that very typical Arab sailor of the ninth century, and in his dominions was to be found the great bird which Sindbad called the roc, as several Arab writers have attested.

When Sri-Vijaya first appears during the seventh century it is in full swing and is recorded as having sent a punitive expedition into Java to quell a rebellion there, and also as sending its ambassadors to China, with which country it can accordingly be assumed that it was trading, because such embassies were sent for diplomatic reasons by all the kingdoms having trade relations with China. From the seventh century Sri-Vijaya rapidly expanded until it became a great maritime empire with wide-flung outposts. As the destiny of South-Eastern Asia depends on the fact that the tide of trade and conquest has flowed from India or Ceylon to the Malay Peninsula and Java, and thence north to China with a reflux west in Champa and Cambodia, and as the Straits of Malacca form the essential passage for that tide, the power which commands those Straits obtains a position of paramountcy. For some six hundred years and more Sri-Vijaya held such a position, and the records tell of the might of its fleet, the prowess of its warriors and sailors, and the fabulous wealth of its Maharajahs derived from the tribute which they extorted from all shipping

THE OLDEST CHRISTIAN CHURCH IN MALAYA
ON THE HILL AT MALACCA

MALACCA IN 1811
From a Picture by I. Wathen

THE OLD GATEWAY, MALACCA, IN 1811
From a Picture by I. Wathen

and traders using the Straits of Malacca. This tribute, we are told, was in the form of gold which was melted into ingots and thrown into a sacred lake in front of the Maharajah's palace.

But Sri-Vijaya was not merely skilled in the arts of war; it was a celebrated centre of Buddhist science and religion, to which Chinese monks resorted to study the holy Sanskrit language, and its Maharajahs were great supporters of the Buddhist faith. The remarkable series of Buddhist monuments in Central Java extends from A.D. 700 to 900, during most of which time the Sailendra Dynasty of Sri-Vijaya was in the ascendancy there, and it was a Maharajah of Sri-Vijaya who caused the temple of Kalasan to be built in A.D. 779. The Borobodur, most renowned of the Sailendra monuments, itself dates from about the middle of the ninth century and is one of the wonders of the world, while in the Temple of Mendoet, near by and dating from the same period, are three statues of Buddha, the face of one of which is said to be the finest piece of work ever wrought by the chisel of a Buddhist artist.

But, though Sri-Vijaya first appears in records during the seventh century A.D. only, the South Indians had been along the Straits of Malacca and on the Malay Peninsula long before then. Before the birth of Christ expeditions by sea had reached Lower Burma and founded settlements there, and had also reached the north of the Malay Peninsula. In the early centuries of our era South Indians had founded settlements in the north of Sumatra and in Kedah, and had crossed the Peninsula and founded others on its eastern coast. Towards the beginning of the Christian era it would seem that two hordes of South Indian invaders from somewhere in Malaysia (more than probably from the shores along the Straits of Malacca) had entered what is Indo-China to-day; one formed the nucleus of the Cham race and the other settled round the delta of the Mekong River. They brought into existence the realm called Fou-Nan by the Chinese, whose early records say that it possessed a very strong navy and comprised what to-day are Cochin-China, Cambodia, Lower Laos, Siam, and much of the eastern part of the Malay Peninsula. Fou-Nan consisted of a number of vassal states under separate princes, each of whom swore allegiance and paid tribute to the central power. Of these vassal states the fiercest and most turbulent were the Cambodian ones, which became joined under one crown towards the end of the fifth century A.D., and wrested the supreme power from Fou-Nan. At about the same time the kingdom of Champa rose to great strength in the region now called Cochin-China, and Fou-Nan disappeared entirely.

Between A.D. 200 and 600 there seems to have been a long period of extreme turbulence in South India, and this possibly accounts for the continual streams of emigrants that were passing into South-Eastern Asia. The Pallava kingdom on the Coromandel coast of India appears in the third century, and had a period of ascendancy from the fourth to the eighth centuries, after which the Cholas became paramount in the same district, and so remained for several centuries. There is the closest connexion between the earliest Indian kingdoms of South-Eastern Asia and the Pallavas.

The earliest traces of the South Indians in the Malaya of to-day date from about A.D. 400, and are to be found in Kedah, Province Wellesley, and Perak. It is clear that there were very ancient Indian settlements near Kedah Peak; where the Sungei Batu Estate is to-day, near Sungei Patani in Kedah; in Province Wellesley, opposite Penang; and at Kuala Selinsing, in Perak. Most interesting remains have been found at all of these places, one of which refers to a great shipowner named Buddha-gupta who flourished at the beginning of the fifth century, and who, having performed a successful sea journey, presented a Buddhist temple as a thank-offering.

By the seventh century A.D. the whole coast from Burma to China and of the islands of the

Malay Archipelago was studded with prosperous Indian colonies and naval stations, while large ships plied regularly between India and China, using these stations as convenient halting-places. Throughout the territory South Indian manners, customs, language, religious practices, learning, and social organizations were to be found.

In the eighth century Sri-Vijaya sent naval expeditions against Champa, and by the beginning of the ninth century we find her the principal maritime power in Malaysia, with an empire that extended over the great part of Sumatra, western and central Java, and the Malay Peninsula, where she had her principal colonies near Kedah Peak on the west coast and round the Bay of Bandon on the east; but during this century her power in Java was shaken by a new dynasty that arose in the centre of that island. In the ninth century, too, there arose a new dynasty of Indian kings in Cambodia that continued through the zenith of Khmer greatness. Its founder, Jayavarman II, whose sacred sword is preserved at Pnom Penh, was a South Indian prince, traditionally said to have come from the Malay Peninsula, and he it was who began in A.D. 860 the building of Angkor city (Angkor Thom), which he completed by the end of that century. Thus the erection of the Borobodur in Java and the beginning of Angkor Thom were more or less synchronous. But dates such as the above mean more when one remembers that the kingdom of Wessex had just become the kingdom of England under half-legendary kings such as Egbert, Ethelwulf, and Alfred, while the Franks were governed by the great Charlemagne, the founder of our Western civilization. Angkor was then already a city apparently of more than a million souls, larger than had been the Athens of Pericles or the Rome of Caesar.

In the tenth and eleventh centuries there was a remarkable outburst of naval activity on the east coast of South India under the strong government of a succession of Chola kings. Rajaraja the Great (985–1016) made himself lord paramount of South India and conquered Kalinga and Ceylon, while under his son, Rajendra I (1012–1043), the Chola power reached its high water mark. We find the Maharajah of Sri-Vijaya in friendly relations with Rajaraja, who allowed him to present a village near Nagapatam for the support of the Buddhist temple at that place, but later on war broke out between Sri-Vijaya and the Cholas. During 1024–1025 Rajendra I sent an overseas expedition against the Maharajah, which was successful. From the inscriptions dealing with this expedition we learn that Sri-Vijaya had a most important station in Kedah called Kataha, or Kadaram, which was an important place containing considerable treasure. We also learn of many other places amongst the 'twelve hundred ancient isles' as Malaysia was called; their names, however, being in Tamil there has been much dispute as to their exact locale, though it is generally agreed that they were in Sumatra and on the Peninsula. Amongst these places perhaps the most intriguing is 'ancient Malaiur, a stronghold situated on a high hill,' and we are at once reminded of Marco Polo's noble city called Malaiur, which unfortunately he never visited. Malaiur is the Tamil version of Malayu, and it seems probable that Malayu was the name which the South Indians gave to Sumatra when they first came there, using a well-known name for their own country. From it, of course, we get Malaya and Malay. Despite the set-back given to it by the great Chola king, Sri-Vijaya soon recovered.

The eleventh and twelfth centuries saw great expansions of the main Indian kingdoms in South-Eastern Asia, and in the first half of the twelfth century the great temple of Angkor Vat was begun. Both here and in Java the imported Indian civilization had by now merged with the indigenous one, and given rise in the former to the Khmer civilization and in the latter to a Hindu-Javanese one that was rapidly passing into the Javanese civilization we know to-day. In the Indian outposts there was no such warfare between Brahmanism and Buddhism as there was in India; the two religions were able to lie peacefully side by side and very largely intermingled. This accounts for the juxtaposition of Buddhist and Brahman temples that are to be found in many places, and for the curious nature of the great temple of Angkor Vat, which for long was considered to have been a Brahman shrine but which the French School of the Far East now considers to have been Buddhist. It certainly is one of the marvels of all time whatever its precise religious significance may have been, and its affinity with the monuments of Central Java is noticeable. The construction of this great temple marked the zenith of Khmer greatness, and the king who built it is usually regarded as the last of the great kings of Cambodia. During his reign there began the disastrous wars between Champa and Cambodia.

The thirteenth century was a period of great disturbance in South-Eastern Asia and witnessed the rise to power of Siam. The great Tartar monarch Kublai Khan was ruling China, and his expeditions of 1254 probably set the Siamese in motion. At all events, in the middle of the thirteenth century they threw off the yoke of Cambodia, and according to their tradition called themselves Thais, meaning free people. It is said that their race started from somewhere in the Chinese province of Yun-nan, and began to settle in what is now Siam at the beginning of the twelfth century A.D., bringing with them a form of Buddhism, and that the modern Buddhism of Cambodia is simply the Siamese form which filtered in about 1250. Modern Siam contains much that is culturally Indian, and there are still Brahmans at the courts in Siam and Cambodia who perform ceremonies and act as astrologers.

In Java the thirteenth century witnessed the rise to supremacy of a purely Javanese dynasty and the downfall of Sri-Vijayan power in that island. Kretanagara, King of Tumapel, began a war against the Sumatran kingdom, which, however, was interrupted by an expedition which the Tartar Emperor Kublai Khan sent against Java to punish it for having cut off the ears of his ambassadors. The expedition was unsuccessful, but it brought temporary respite to Sri-Vijaya, which during the same century had planted a colony on the island of Tamsak or Tamasak, and had founded there a settlement called by the Sanskrit name of Singhapura, the City of the Lion, in which connexion it may be remembered that one of the earliest Sri-Vijayan inscriptions called its king the 'Royal Lion.' This settlement seems to have flourished greatly for more than a hundred years and to have had five kings, all of whom bore Indian names. It has been the fashion locally to record Singapore as having been founded by a prince of 'the ancient Malay kingdom of Palembang,' but it seems that the name Palembang was not used until after Sri-Vijaya had been conquered. Moreover, this last was not a Malay kingdom at all, as we understand that expression nowadays; it was culturally Indian, as every description of it plainly shows, though the common people were doubtless Malays.

It would seem that ancient Singhapura was founded somewhere about A.D. 1250, and that it had been conquered by the Javanese of Majapahit by 1365. It must have been a place of considerable importance, but it is strange that neither the name Singhapura nor any phonetic equivalent of it appears in any of the records until one gets it in the earliest Portuguese books at the beginning of the sixteenth century. Such references as there are in Chinese give either the Chinese equivalent of Tamasak or the Chinese name for the Straits of Singapore. The Arabs give nothing before 1554 that can be referred with certainty to the place, though some authors find references under names which outwardly appear to have nothing to do with it at all.

The fourteenth century saw the final downfall of Sri-Vijaya and its colony Singhapura before the conquering Javanese, while further east the Annamites conquered Champa, whose king fled to Java, and the Siamese wrested more and more territory from the Khmers, finally driving them with terrible slaughter from Angkor in the fifteenth century when the city and its great temple gradually became smothered in the jungle, from which it has been rescued only comparatively recently. The Siamese in the fourteenth century had extended their conquests right down to the south of the Malay Peninsula, and had unsuccessfully attacked Singhapura by sea before that place fell to the Javanese.

Islam penetrated into Malaysia with the Arabs, and by the beginning of the sixteenth century had triumphed everywhere, so that in 1526 the last Indian Brahmans went to Bali, where you will find their religious and other customs very much to-day as they were in that century. We can say, then, that by the beginning of the sixteenth century the Indian civilization of South-Eastern Asia was stamped out, but it continued and still continues to exert the strongest influence.

Taking our own Malay civilization we find traces of the old South Indians remaining in the Sanskrit and Tamil words incorporated into the Malay language. Sanskrit was, of course, the language of Buddhism and of the royal courts and officials. Tamil merchants and sailors made their words so important that you find that the Malay words for ship (*kapal*) and boat (*prahu*) and for shop (*kedei*) and warehouse (*gedong*, or godown, as we call it to-day) are all Tamil, as are many other words relating to trade. Dr. Winstedt has written that 'the more one studies the subject, the more one realizes the immense debt Malaya owes to India for folk-tales as well as for language, religion, custom, literature, and general culture'; and as it is with Malaya, so it is with all the rest of South-Eastern Asia.

The tiger was the emblem of the great Chola kings of South India, and it is fitting that the tiger should be Malaya's emblem to-day. Our Malay Sultans proudly trace their ancestry to Alexander the Great through an Indian prince Sang Sapurba, son of Raja Suran, the Ruler of the East and West, by his marriage with a mermaid, daughter of the Kings of the Sea. This prince revealed himself on the hill of Seguntang in the hinterland of Palembang.

This tradition contains much truth. Alexander the Great was doubtless introduced into the story through the influence of Arab and Persian tradition after Malaya turned Islam, but that the Malay Sultans are descended from some Indian prince or princes is so probable as in my view to be almost certain, and it is to Sri-Vijaya that one must go for the original ancestor. The earliest records of this kingdom have been discovered within recent years at the foot of and near the hill of Seguntang; and this is probably the mountain of which the Maharajahs of Sri-Vijaya claimed to be the lords. Certain it is that for more than six hundred years the Great Maharajah, King of the Mountain, played a tremendous part in the creation of the Malay civilization which we know to-day.

FRANCES BARBER

WHENEVER I go to Malacca there is one pilgrimage that I always make. In the evening when the sun is working down-stage to the bravado of his exit, I climb to the top of the Hill and sit under the old pommeloe tree by the flag-staff with Frances Barber.

Who is she? Well, she's been a sweetheart of mine for a very long time, and she was, so I believe, the first-known Englishwoman to be buried in Malaya. Actually she was 'the most pious wife' of Captain James Barber, and she died in childbirth on September 10, 1695, while she was accompanying her husband on a voyage from the Island of Bombay to China. The tombstone does not say that she was English, but I know that she was, and I know just what she looked like and what she thought about things, and indeed all about her, and I'll tell you how I know.

The first time I went into the old Portuguese Church on the top of the Hill at Malacca I very nearly put my foot on Frances Barber's stone, which until quite recently was one of three that lay right at the threshold of the church entrance.

Something, however, caused me to look down, and, with foot poised, I read the quaint old Latin inscription, then stepped back and walked around into the church. But I had to come back immediately and read that inscription again, so much had it intrigued me. It was there and then that I first met Mistress Barber; and she curtsyed and laughed into my eyes.

Many and many are the times since then that she and I have talked together as we watched the sun westering to England, and sometimes I used to be depressed and downhearted, which is an effect the setting sun frequently produces in the heart of an exile. But always her courage, her strength, and her common sense have coaxed me out of my blues; and when, as more often, I have been feeling happy, she has just bubbled over with fun and sent me off to my dinner feeling like a million dollars.

Frances was not one of your thick-thighed, deep-bosomed, broad-hipped, peasant-healthy women; or would she have died in childbirth? No, sir, she was a little fairy of a woman, one of those little women of steel courage and lion heart; or would she otherwise have braved the uncharted seas, the stifling cabin, the discomfort and danger of that voyage from Bombay to be with her man? Her hair was the colour of ripened wheat and her eyes of the English Channel; her hand was firm and cool, as I know, for often it has lain in mine. Her voice was clear and sweet, and every one had to love her, even the stolid Dutch, for does not her stone tell how they laboured and strove to save her life, those '*Batavi, genus hospitale*'?

As I said before, well-meaning hands have recently moved the stone of Frances Barber, but she is not pleased about that, although it was kindly meant. She preferred it where it used to lie, beside that of another woman who died in childbirth. This latter was Mevrouw Sophia Hengelbosch, beloved wife of the noble Heer Pieter van Resselaar, Governor and Director of the Town and Fortress of Malacca; and the stone also commemorates the husband's death. A most swanky pair to have beside one. On the other side was George Cooke, who had been Captain of a Dutch vessel and had died on his way back from China in 1712; of him it was recorded that he was 'endowed with various kinds of knowledge,' as indeed befitted one who had to go down to the sea in ships at that period. Opposite the church and leaning against the Residency wall were two old Malay tombstones dating from the fifteenth century. So there we had a lot of history—Malay, Portuguese, Dutch, English, indeed a history of Malacca; and amongst the dreams that Frances and I dream together our favourites are about old Malacca.

The first scene that she and I are wont to picture is that of a small village inhabited by a primitive race of fishermen; its only street consists of a few shanties and its visible wealth lies tied up at the mouth of the river, a cluster of rude dug-outs. It is the village of Malacca six hundred years ago.

We rub our eyes, and into it have poured the flotsam and jetsam of the cruel Javanese war, the poor hunted creatures who have come from many parts, but particularly from Palembang and Singapore, reduced now to ruins and ashes, and drenched in blood. The little village of Malacca has now begun to live, has acquired a bustle that it never knew before. Huts are springing up to right and left, fresh clearings are eating into the jungle, and alongside the dug-outs there now lie the larger boats in which the refugees arrived. The fish are learning to fear the line and hook, where before they only knew the spear; the land is beginning to yield its proper burden of fruit and food. Civilization has dawned on the little village and its rude inhabitants.

Malacca to-day is and long has been the Brighton of the Chinese in Malaya. One is too apt to regard them carelessly as immigrants attracted by our flag and having no traditions in the country; but that is all wrong. China was the great overlord of the seas and countries of

Malaya in the long-gone days when universal dominion was the tradition of an Emperor appointed by Heaven to be the ruler of the whole earth. From the fifth century after Christ, when the Buddhist pilgrim Fa-hsien entered Java, the Chinese came in ever-increasing numbers and penetrated farther with each voyage.

So we rub our eyes once more and open them at the beginning of the fifteenth century, when the great Ming Dynasty had brought to China a new era of peace and commerce. The village has grown by now into a small town. The river is spanned by a fair-sized bridge on which are twenty small shops, where a lively trade proceeds. The money in use is made from tin; the bargain is effected by pointing to heaven, and no writing is used to bind it. The houses in the town are numerous and they are made of wood, raised from the ground on piles, with their floors covered by cane matting; houses, indeed, just such as you can see to-day in the outskirts of Malacca. The whole town is enclosed within a wooden wall, for tigers abound, and in the wall are four gates with watch-towers where the drum beats to mark the divisions of the day or to give the alarm.

To this very day if you want to ask the time in Malay you say *Pukul b'rapa*? (How many times has it beaten?), and the answer will be *Sudah pukul ampat* (It has beaten four), or whatever the number of the hour may be; while outside all police stations there still hangs a metal gong on which the hour is beaten.

Law and order have come to Malacca and at night a patrol goes round the streets with bells ringing. Inside the outer wall, and well into the town, there is a palisaded fortress within which lie the wealth and food of the population stored in godowns. The prosperity of the place rests on its tin industry, which is reasonably well organized, the two principal mines being controlled by officers appointed by the king, and the smelted tin being made into ingots of standard weight.

The few streets are buzzing with excitement; Chinese soldiers and sailors are to be seen everywhere, and a roaring trade is going on. Out in the harbour lies a fleet of junks which have brought the Chinese ambassador, the great eunuch Cheng Ho, with a large entourage and an army of men. Having acquired military merit his Emperor had raised him to the position of First Eunuch, and now has sent him on the first of many embassies. See, there is a violent stir in the street, and people from all sides run to watch the passing of a stream of armed Malays who surround a sedan-chair in which is seated the King of Malacca. Round his head is a fine white cloth of native cotton, on his body a long robe of flowered green material, and on his feet sandals of leather. He is on his way to see Cheng Ho, and what they say to each other will be interpreted by two Chinese Mohammedan priests, who can speak Malay and know the Arabic language. They have left us accounts of their adventures.

Cheng Ho's mission was splendidly successful; he took back with him envoys from Malacca and returned later with an inscribed stone which he set up on the Hill to record the fact that henceforth the place lay under the protection of China. And so it remained for a hundred years; its kings paid frequent visits to the court of the Emperor, where they were treated handsomely and received magnificent gifts in return for a tribute which as Malacca grew more and more prosperous came to include agate, pearls, tortoise-shell, coral trees, birds' nests, rhinoceros horns, ivory, black bears, black monkeys, parrots, camphor, rose-oil, gums, spices, gold, and precious stones. You can find it all written in the Chronicles of the Ming Dynasty, but the historian cynically adds that what China spent 'was not little either.'

A wonderful man this eunuch Cheng Ho, or Sam-po as he is better known to-day; three Emperors he served and seven times did he conduct embassies through the Southern Seas, where his name became a word of power so that subsequent envoys would use it to clinch their diplomacies. His voyages are spoken of in the Chinese records as the greatest event of the Ming Dynasty ; and after his death the Emperor deified him, so that to-day as Sam-po he is one of the gods of China. In Malacca there is a hill which the Malays call *Bukit China* (Chinese Hill), but which the Chinese call Sam-po's Hill. At its foot you will find the Sam-po Kong, an old temple founded in A.D. 1796, and built in front of an ancient well from which tradition says Sam-po's men took their water when his fleet visited Malacca. Behind the altar are two little figures, one, the smaller, depicting Sam-po in life, the other, the larger, behind and above the first, depicting him after deification.

To me, Cheng Ho seems to be one of the greatest adventurers who ever sailed through the Straits of Malacca, and worthy to be remembered with Albuquerque and Houtman, Drake and Lancaster. The last of the masters whom he served so well created for him the special post of Guardian of Nanking, and, while holding it, he died.

When next we see Malacca it is in the year 1511 ; the fleet of the great Alfonso Albuquerque is already at sea but has not yet arrived, and the town is unaware of its coming fate. Sultan Mahmud Shah, grandson of the great Mansur Shah, is on the throne, and the town has become one of the best-known trading ports of the Old

World. Yet it is not in reality a trading city; it is rather the site of a vast fair where East barters with West. The town has, of course, grown enormously since last we saw it; the streets are thronged with merchants and hangers-on and adventurers from every race in the East; the harbour is full of shipping, to which there is a constant hurrying to and fro of row-boats.

In the part of the town which lies to the south of the river are the houses of the Malay nobles, the Mosque, and the Sultan's palace, a large building roofed with tiles which Cheng Ho had brought from China. In this part the buildings are of stone and mortar, but across the river to the north, where the city is most extensive and the merchants dwell, the houses are of wood with thatched roofs. The Sultan keeps a great display of soldiers as a precaution, for he lives entirely on the toll levied from the traders, and his government is as completely wicked as he is himself. The Chinese merchants from the ships live in a large inn where they are waited on by female slaves. A visitor has written sardonically that the proprietor used to send food and drink each morning to his guests, 'but if one uses too freely of this, he may be sure that all his money will pass into the hands of others.' Ludovico di Varthema, the Bolognese traveller who was in Malacca at the beginning of the sixteenth century, wrote that 'it is not possible to go about the place here when it is dark, because people are killed like dogs, and all the merchants who arrive here by ship go to sleep in their ships.' He depicts Malacca as an evil place and the Malays as an evil race. 'The King keeps a governor to administer justice for foreigners, but those of the country take the law into their own hands, and they are the worst race that was ever created on earth.'

Prosperous and busy though the town appears to be, the sun of the Malay Sultans of Malacca that has been for some time on the wane is now just about to sink below the horizon. Since we last saw the little town at the beginning of the fifteenth century it has passed through the Augustan era of Mansur Shah; its Sultans made rich by its trade were able to fit out armies of conquest and make themselves masters of Pahang, Kampar, Siak, and Indragiri; its laws had been framed, its municipality organized, and its institutions settled; it had embraced a new faith and become Mohammedan. But now this golden age has passed, its heroes are all dead; Hang Tuah, the Admirable Crichton of ancient Malaya, who knew a good kris by its look and counted his loves by the hundred, has gone to the Prophet, and the Sultan who now reigns is an evil beast. Three men there had been and three only who might have saved

Malacca from the Portuguese—the Bendahara (Viceroy) and his two sons, the commanders-in-chief of the fleet and the army, but the Sultan had had them put to death. The episode is typical of him and of the evil days upon which Malacca had fallen. The Bendahara had a very beautiful daughter, Fatimah, whom the Sultan first saw at her wedding and whom he at once courted, nursing thereafter a grievance against the Bendahara for having refused to allow him to see her before. Seizing on an accusation of treason and conspiracy against the throne, the Sultan sent two of his nobles with a kris on a silver platter as a token to the Bendahara that 'the power of fate had reached him.' After his death, the Sultan had his two sons and the unhappy husband of Fatimah put to death, and then took to wife the coveted beauty.

So when Albuquerque's trumpets sounded on the Feast of St. James in 1511 there were no strong leaders left in Malacca, and the town fell to the Portuguese after a few days' struggle. But let that not detract from Albuquerque's feat of arms, for with seven hundred Europeans he stormed walls and entrenchments that were guarded by thirty thousand men and many cannons. For long thereafter the Portuguese fought off attack after attack by the Malay Sultans who, after they were driven from Malacca, founded another Sultanate in Johore. You can judge what tough men these Portuguese soldiers must have been from the brass helmet that is to be seen in the Malacca Room at Raffles Museum. Just fancy fighting in that during the blaze of a Malayan sun!

At the next shake of our kaleidoscope Frances and I see a town that is entirely changed, for now we jump one hundred and thirty years and it is 1641.

As we now sit on the Hill we see at our feet a square stone fortress five stories high built out on to the very sea itself so as to ensure victualling in time of siege. This fortress stood where the Hong-Kong and Shanghai Bank now stands, as the contractor for the latter building found to his very great profit. A stone wall twenty feet high and proportionately broad runs round the Hill, enclosing the Portuguese part of the town. Within this wall are the Governor's Palace, the Bishop's Palace, the State Council Hall, the Hall of the Brotherhood of Mercy, a cathedral and four other churches, and two hospitals. There are only seven and a half thousand Christians in the whole of Malacca at this time, but nevertheless there are four religious houses, eight parishes, fourteen churches, two Chapters of the Hospitallers, and some hermitages and oratories. Verily, as a contemporary English book has it, 'the

Portingals live after the manner of their country with a Bishop and a college of Jesuits besides the Castell.'

Malacca as a trading place has long since fallen from its high estate, for the Portuguese by their foolish policies and their rapacity have all but killed its trade. They themselves have deteriorated terribly by intermarriage with the Asiatics, and morality has fallen to a very low ebb. Even in the time of St. Francis Xavier, who once lay buried in the old church beside which we sit, the Portuguese had fallen into evil ways, for during his first visit in 1547 he scourged the inhabitants for their vices and their crimes. On his final departure for Japan, where he died, he publicly cursed Malacca. Standing at the church door, the Saint took off his sandals, struck from them the dust, and declaring the place accursed, refused to bear away with him so much as even the dust from the earth. Dreadful scandals occurred in Malacca, and to this day the natives believe that the ghosts of a nun and a soldier meet nightly on the slopes of the old Hill to carry out an ancient tryst. Both had been put to death, so tradition says, for incontinency; and one of our Judges used often to tell the story of how, when he was in Malacca holding Assizes, his boy came dashing in one evening scared to death because he had seen a man in what he called *pakeian kerosine*, which means clothes like a kerosene tin!

By 1641 a tremendous change has come over the balance of European sea-power. The huge wealth that poured into Europe from the Indies (as Malaysia was then called) had aroused the cupidity of the great Catholic powers of Spain and Portugal. In 1492 the Genoese Columbus, in the pay of the King of Spain, sailed west in order to prove the theory which he had formed in 1474 that the way to the Indies lay westward. In 1497 the Portuguese Vasco da Gama had rounded the Cape and ravaged the Indian Ocean. Tremendous wealth had poured into Spain from America and into Portugal from Malaysia and India, and the navies of these two countries held the sea-power of Europe for long, but the Protestant sailors of England and the Dutch Republic began to make things uncomfortable for them towards the end of the sixteenth century. In 1580 the Dutch Republic declared its independence and began its long fight to free itself from Spain. In 1588 the English defeated the Spanish Armada, and thereafter the Dutch Republic finally gained its independence. The sea-power of Spain was broken, and the Protestant seamen began to turn their faces to the East Indies. Exploratory voyages were undertaken; and first the Dutch and then the English formed their East India Companies. We only

THE OLD DUTCH STADT-HOUSE, MALACCA

GEORGETOWN, PENANG, IN 1811

From a Picture by I. Wathen

turned to India proper when our early Malayan enterprise had proved unsuccessful; thus the Indian Empire was the direct offspring of Malayan trade. The Dutch prospered more than the English; they drove the principal Portuguese garrisons out of the islands of the Archipelago, but their first attempts upon the greatest prize, Malacca, failed, and naval defeats were inflicted upon them by the Portuguese. Then they began a general blockage of Malacca which lasted for ten years until, at the beginning of June 1640, they invested the town so rigorously and so closely that its supply of victuals was entirely cut off. In July they began a siege of the town that lasted until, on January 14, 1641, they finally stormed the place at daybreak and captured it.

And so we come to the last view that Frances and I can take together of the little town. It is 1695, and Malacca is now very Dutch, with square-sterned Burghers walking its streets. Captain Barber's small ship lies out in the harbour, but my little friend, alas! lies on her death-bed in the house of some kind Dutch people. Always when we reach this last scene Frances gives a wry little smile and a final squeeze of my hand as I hear her whisper, 'Never mind, it was all well worth it, for I loved and I was happy.' Then she goes, the sun goes, and I go.

Malacca is still very Dutch with its old church built by pious Burghers in 1753, a wonderful structure with ceiling beams hewn solid out of great Malayan trees and carrying a span of level ceiling that no modern architect would attempt. It contains the finest example of a total lack of humour that I know. You will see a simply colossal tombstone, made of a solid slab of granite, and you will read that it is 'a slight token of respect' for the corpse underneath. How the poor soul will ever get out when Gabriel sounds the last alarm, I do not know.

Near the church is the quaint old Dutch Stadt-house, which now houses some Government offices and the Supreme Court when it sits in Malacca; mind you go through it, for it contains some fine old woodwork and it will interest you. In the narrow streets you will come across more than a few of the old Dutch houses, and there is a very find old Chinese temple[1] that dates back a long way, and that contains the ancestral tablets of the oldest Chinese families of Malaya, while in the country you will find beautiful views and lovely green ricefields (I know none more lovely) with many a fine Malay house built of wood in the classic Malay style. And there are heaps of other jolly things that you can discover for yourself as you

[1] The Cheng Hoon Teng Temple described in 'Many Gods,' page 68 f.

walk about the streets or drive along the country roads.

So please do pay a visit to old Malacca and turn back the centuries, for, believe me, in that quiet little town a mighty past keeps watch and ward to-day.

A TRAGEDY OF JOHN COMPANY

IT is half-past two in the morning and I am in for a *nuit blanche*. They have been dancing in the hotel to-night, and the tunes still throb in my head. Outside, the rain is falling; I hear it crackle through the fronds of the coco-nut beside my eyrie. The motor-cars have long since departed, and the street is slumbering. The only sounds are the rain and the clip-clop, clip-clop of clogged feet wending homeward.

But the rain and the mystery of those passing feet set my mind thinking of the lost chances and old unhappinesses of life, and of feet that passed more than a hundred years ago, the feet of one who like me took the law for his mistress. He died of a broken heart; died by his own hand and the tongue of slander, for he was young enough to dare death but too young to brave the malice of his fellows. The bare facts of his tragedy are to be found entombed in one of our local law reports,[1] but I will give you the story in the way that my imagination for long has depicted it.

It is a story of Prince of Wales' Island, the

[1] See Kyshe's *Ecclesiastical Reports*, p. 1.

old Penang of John Company, at the time of sicca rupees, cocked hats, subontadars, silver dragon-headed sticks, umbrellas of ceremony, and all the rest of the snobbish flummery of officialdom in those days.

To me Penang always suggests the John Company of the early nineteenth century. Much of the original town is still to be seen in the modern one, though each passing year sees less; then there is the Royal coat of arms in the Supreme Court with its White Horse of Hanover; and opposite the Court House is the little white Church of St. George the Martyr. This is a favourite of mine that I often visit, and that invariably gives me an inward chuckle. Why? Well, the black commemorative tablet is the cause. It tells us that the foundation-stone of the Church was laid in 1817 'by the munificence of the East India Company, under the auspices of the Governor, W. E. Phillipps, Esquire'; while in the following year 'under the administration of his successor, Colonel Alexander Bannerman, the edifice was completed by Captain R. Smith, Engineer.' No nonsense, you see, about the glory of God; just the glory of the Esquire, the Colonel, and the Engineer, and the munificence of good old John Company. I only visit the little church when it is empty, but for me its emptiness is filled with ghostly uniforms and nankeen trousers and billowy satins and silks, and in the pulpit I see some long-forgotten Rev. Mr. Honeyman, oiled and curled, with his thoughts on a couple of bottles of port at the Governor's table in Suffolk House after the tiresome business is done.

By the way, somebody asked me the other day why the East India Company was called John Company, and you, too, may want to know. The answer is not too certain, but the best explanation is that it was the native attempt at pronouncing Hon. Company, which was the way the Company was so often described in official documents and proclamations.

Well, my story opens at the close of 1808. Georgetown then is a very small, very beautiful place. The harbour of clear water shelters fine-sparred ships, a sandy beach runs a silver ribbon round the island, and from the jetty a white road winds to lose itself at the foot of the Hill, clothed with betel palms and all the wonderful forestry of Malaya. The town itself is, perhaps, more seafaring than mercantile; punch-houses and brothels obtrude too frequent heads. The nights, too often, are made hideous by the brawling and fighting of drunken seamen ashore after a long, uncomfortable, and arduous voyage.

In 1807 the King had granted a Charter of Justice to the island, and the first Recorder of the new Court has now arrived, Sir Edmond Stanley.

The Europeans of the town are already cloven by him into factions and cliques. The covenanted merchants and officials had been used to having matters all their own way; justice had been Executive justice, and those covenanted Europeans who were not officials had been more or less outside the law. Descends amongst them this Irish Recorder, looking for trouble and finding it; hot-headed, hot-tongued, violent-tempered, too keenly sensitive of the dignity of himself and his Court, he has reacted on Penang as a stick thrust into an ant-heap. Perhaps you cannot blame him too much; his task is a difficult one, needing the greatest tact and courtesy. But the man chosen is Irish, trained in that school of advocates that conducted at its own personal risk the treason trials after the Rebellion of 1798; several years of service in the Irish Parliament have not taught him toleration, his promotion to the high position of Prime Serjeant-at-law of His Majesty in Ireland has not given him humility. It is more than likely that he was swollen-headed; it is very certain that he was hasty and injudicious. As soon as he set foot on the island he fell foul of the Governor and the officials, and so commenced a quarrel between the Court and the Executive which lasted to the days of the last Recorder and only finished (if it has yet) with Crown Colony Government.

But he was not altogether to blame; the sort of thing which had been going on in Penang is illustrated by the revelations in one of the first cases which he tried. An unfortunate Indian butler who served the Colonel of the 20th Bengal Native Infantry had received twenty strokes of the rattan for some petty offence. He complained to the civil Magistrate, who took no steps beyond advising the Colonel. The butler was tied to a stake in the presence of the whole battalion and received one hundred lashes with the cat-o'-nine-tails on the plea that he had traduced the Colonel by representing him as a bad master; he was then put in the cells for two and a half months. When he came out, he brought an action against the Colonel in the Recorder's Court, and Sir Edmond Stanley awarded him one hundred and fifty dollars. Now, an island where Colonels are allowed publicly to commit injustice, where the civil Magistrate is hand in glove with his brother officials to the burking of complaints against them, was hardly one which would welcome the intervention of the strong arm of justice. Intrigues against the Recorder were as rife as the causes which he gave for just offence.

Into this turmoil there came in 1809 a young lawyer named Thomas Kekewich, then only twenty-five, having been born at Islington in

1784. His brother George was Judge Advocate of the Cape Colony in 1813, and his cousin aide-de-camp in the same year to the General at Colombo; he himself says in his will that he came of respectable parentage and that he had received the education of a gentleman. Beyond that I know nothing of his people, but his type is easy to place. He came of one of those families that have done all the hard work of the Empire for the last two hundred years, but now are being taxed and badgered out of existence. They breed professional men, divines, soldiers, sailors, and civil servants; their standard is that of the English gentleman, their brains perhaps are not always of the very highest, but they have plenty of common sense, and, being good sportsmen, their honesty and candour is beyond reproach.

After some difficulty Thomas Kekewich is admitted to practise as a special law agent; he places his board outside a small shop-house, on the top floor of which he has his office, and waits for the oyster of prosperity to open. He takes a neat little house in the country and obtains the services of a faithful servant named Boloo; for companions he has his dogs and cats. He is only a young unknown lawyer with no introductions of any moment, and he finds that the officials take no notice of him and the merchants but little, so that when he came to make his will he stated that from only two of the latter had he received kindness. But he is too sensitive, too highly strung, too lonely a man to attract to himself friendships ; and he is far too proud to try and push himself into society. So he goes on his quiet way, out in the early morning and evening with his dogs, playing cribbage with his friends Daniel Jones, the Registrar of the Court, and Richard Caunter, the Police Magistrate. He spends much time reading and more writing ; he sees a certain amount of social life at the hospitable home of the Caunter family, with whom he is on the closest terms, but his greatest delights come when the fat crossed and recrossed letters arrive from England and he hears of the doings of his mother and his old nurse, Ann Swanston, and his nephew and all the rest of them. These letters must be read and reread and puzzled over, for the thin writing is not too easy to follow ; and when they are mastered there will be happy evenings spent in answering them, when all his small doings will find a greater interest and he will doubtless be forced to balance his accounts with himself. Thus he is happy and contented ; he finds, too, that the clients are beginning to come in and the fee book to fill in an encouraging way. His letters home begin to show the feel of coming success, the gods seem as if they smile, when suddenly there falls a bolt from the blue and a beginning is made of the end.

Not content to quarrel with every one else, the Recorder has now begun to fall foul of his Bar. The first to come under his grinding heel is Mr. Cuthbert Fenwick, whom he commits to gaol in May 1810. In endeavouring to procure the release of some native clients from a custody which he is seeking to prove illegal, Mr. Fenwick has filed a petition containing what the Recorder holds to be reflections upon the administration of justice by himself. So to gaol with Mr. Fenwick, who, though he is a high-spirited man and courageous, can only stand a week of the noxious filthy place and craves for pardon. He is released because of 'the crowded state of the gaol,' as the Recorder puts it in the order.

The next victim is Thomas Kekewich. He is sitting in his office one morning at the beginning of June 1810 when a Mohammedan Indian comes in and pours out a long grievance. It takes much time to unravel and contains interminable irrelevances and an inflexible determination to evade totally the points involved, but at last Tom has got to the bottom of it all. The man seems to have a reasonable grievance, the fee is paid, the client departs as volubly as he came, and Tom settles down to draft the petition, which he finds involves certain pleas concerning the actions of Mr. Young, the Senior Sworn Clerk of the Court. At last the draft is complete, it is engrossed and sent off to the Court to be filed; the afternoon being on the decline the lawyer puts on his hat, locks his office, and walks home happy to his dinner and his dogs and his books.

A week or so later he finds himself called upon to answer for his conduct in having dared to make statements concerning an officer of the Court, statements which the Recorder says are libels on the Court. White with rage at the injustice and bravely guarding the interests of his client, Kekewich tells the Recorder that if necessary he will go to gaol for life rather than withdraw the statements in the petition and apologize for them; so to gaol he goes, and while he lies there more trouble occurs in Court.

For some time the High Constables, who are respectable English merchants, have been in a state of revolt; the Recorder has so worked on them that in July they come into Court during the Assizes and resign in a body. The Recorder is furious, and thunders at Mr. David Brown of Glugor, the High Sheriff, to restore order. That gentleman rises from his seat and tells the Recorder that he too will not act any longer. Mr. John Dunbar (a name remembered in the mercantile annals of Penang) then tells the

Recorder that, while the Court is conducted as it is and matters are allowed to go on as they are, it is, in his opinion, a danger and a disgrace to remain a High Constable. The Court is reduced to a complete state of disorder and confusion, and so adjourns.

The Recorder drives off to Government House where he eats humble pie, and the next time he mounts the bench it is in company with the Governor, who smoothes matters over.

For a long month Tom Kekewich lies in gaol until at length his health breaks down, his will gives way and he apologizes and is set at liberty. His name is restored to the rolls of the Court in August, but his health is so broken that he lies ill in his house for a long time, and when he has recovered he finds that all his money has gone and he is in debt. The clients are very shy now, for they say his name is unlucky, and he gets so little work that he sinks deeper into the financial mire; and when his best friend Daniel Jones, the Registrar of the Court, dies in April 1811, the cup of his sorrow seems filled almost to overflowing.

But he is offered the vacant position and in May he accepts it, and, going to serve under the Recorder, the fly steps into the spider's web.

The burden of debt hangs round poor Tom like a millstone and, as the months slip away, it grows rather than decreases, so that at his wit's end he commits an act in October 1811, which is the ultimate cause of his end. What actually happened or where the exact blame lay we do not know nor ever shall, but this is how he referred to it in January 1813, shortly before his death. 'While a clerk in the office of Sir Edmond Stanley, the Recorder, and Registrar of the Court, led on by that bad man to share in the spoils, I did a deed that has ever since destroyed my peace of mind, and I will boast that it is the only evil deed I can accuse myself of while in that situation, and I have severely suffered for it for fifteen months, the destructive tooth of a self-accusing conscience has preyed upon my weak frame; nor day nor night, have I ever known one moment's ease. The deed has been discovered! and that evil-minded villain is about to publish it to the world, and throwing all off his own shoulders to make me alone the guilty wretch.'

Long before he wrote these words, the Recorder and a Scottish doctor had been putting it about Penang that Tom was a runaway from his country and a detested outcast from his family, but Tom had kept his 'large Europe leather trunk' filled with his cherished letters from home, and in his will directed his executors to that trunk as containing a full refutation of such charges.

Whether the Recorder was guilty of corruption

or not, it is certain that he passed on with honour from Penang to Madras, where he became Chief Justice, eventually retiring in 1825 and dying at Richmond in 1843.

From the time of his lapse Tom's health gradually failed; he grew more and more morose, more bitterly self-contained, until in September 1812 he resigned his position as Registrar since his health precluded him from its duties. Scandal had spread and spread and he knew full well that when his evil deed was finally exposed he would have to face the blame, and the Recorder would be secure in his high position. Prosperity and health already gone, reputation was about to follow them finally; life seemed to hold nothing more for him, and death to be his only escape from the intolerable burdens of Fate.

One night he picks up his pistol to clean it, and as he turns it over in his hand he determines that it shall be the means of escape. It is the twenty-fourth of October 1812, and the rain is pouring outside, the bull-frogs raise their dreadful voices, the world seems drenched in tears; and despair, blank and utter, seizes him. He goes into his bedroom and seats himself at his desk, where he writes his will, no ordinary document but the cry of a defeated soul 'meaning soon to leave this world of care and trouble.'

As the pen flows there comes to him the

thought of the idiotic barbarities perpetrated in those days upon the body of a *felo de se*; and so he writes: 'If it should be thought fit to bury me in a cross-road, with a stake driven through me, and to act all the mummery that is usually performed against those that choose to seek Heaven by their own hands, rather than to live the scoff of a base degenerated world, be it so. This is a good piece of priestcraft to frighten old nurses and children. I laugh at it, for I have never been able to discover how the abuse of a stinking dead body can affect a man's immortal part.'

For long minutes the sounds of the rain, the bull-frogs, and the scratching quill continue, until at last the will is signed and sealed, for in those days no witnesses were required.

He picks up the pistol and has started to load it when the good Boloo comes in with his evening night-cap and stays to chat awhile about those petty things that are always so important to native servants. The interruption, however, serves a purpose which Boloo could never have guessed, for with his departure Tom's thoughts are changed. He puts the pistol back and places the will in his desk, then takes his drink, undresses, and climbs wearily into bed. The rain suddenly stops, as tropical rain will, and the voices of the bull-frogs that had seemed so harsh and mocking now grow softly monotonous until at last they sound a lullaby and Tom's poor soul drifts into the peace of sleep.

But matters go from worse to worse; the weeks drag by; Christmas comes, a momentary glimpse of happiness at the Caunters' home; the New Year bustles in with fire-crackers and the clink of spoons against punch-bowls, but it has nothing to offer Tom.

On the thirtieth of January 1813, he adds a codicil to his will. More weeks drag by; the outlook now is at its blackest, his trouble is just about to become open and public.

It is the eighteenth of March 1813. Once more the rain crashes down in torrents, the harsh croakings outside sound like voices calling to him from hell. He takes up his pistol, loads it, and Boloo dashes in a moment later to find his master dead. Outside in the compound the dogs are howling, for they have sensed what has happened. Good faithful dogs. Here is what Tom had written of them in his will: 'I have four dogs that are named Griffin, Punch, Dash, and Toby; and two cats, Tibby and Titty. I hope my Executors will excuse my weakness in requesting that these animals may be taken care of. Dogs won't slander you; dogs never tell infamous lies, but are open and candid; therefore don't let these faithful servants be cast away.'

And with those kind words of his we may

leave poor Tom, a tragedy of John Company, and merely add that the verdict of a sympathetic jury enabled him to be buried in the little old cemetery in Penang where Francis Light, its founder, lies. Drop a kindly tear as you pass it on your way to the hotel.

DEAD-LINE

WHEN the journalist calls it a day and grabs for his hat, he thanks the gods of ink for the dead-line; but, if he is a good journalist, that same dead-line leaves him dissatisfied and conscious that his work might have been so much better, so much brighter than it was; and that is how I feel as I come to this last piece. Singapore is such an interesting place, so little understood outside and so little appreciated inside, that it really is worth writing about. For my part, I have only attempted to give you a background against which you can paint your own picture; but the place does merit one really good book, and some day that book will be written, some unknown Kipling will rise in our midst and tell the world.

Until then we must rely on those who, like me, are in the direct line of Bat'h, as the Malays call their legendary herald, from whom are descended the reciters of their ancient histories. My grandfather was, for his time, a great Malay scholar and also an enthusiastic historian. As a small boy I remember the tin cases which he kept full of his notes about Malaya, notes written in

Chinese account books in a curious kind of shorthand which he invented, and which only the late Mr. C. B. Buckley could read after his death. All these notes my father sent to Mr. Buckley, and they duly formed the basis of his *Anecdotal History of Singapore*, but unluckily they were all destroyed in a fire which occurred in Mr. Buckley's office, so that masses of material relating to other parts of Malaya were lost.

Not only did I hear much about Singapore and Malaya from my grandfather during our Sunday walks and often when I sat with him after dinner, but when I came back to Singapore old Mr. Buckley and the late Major St. Clair of the *Singapore Free Press* took me under their wings and I learnt plenty more. Then when the centenary was being celebrated I took part in the editing and writing of the memorial history called *One Hundred Years of Singapore*. Added to all of which is the fact that for the past many years I have been a close student of all available material written in English or French concerning the ancient history of Malaysia and South-Eastern Asia—German and Dutch, unfortunately, I cannot read—so, as I said before, I can claim to be of the sons of Bat'h.

It looks as though a long connexion with the Straits Settlements will end with me, a connexion that began when my grandfather came to Penang in 1844. He was then a sugar-planter, but when his venture failed he joined the East India Company's service on January 1, 1849. In 1859 he was called to the Bar at Gray's Inn, and in 1862 he retired from the East India Company and began to practise at the Bar in Singapore, since when there have been Braddells in this city continuously; but with me it seems that we shall reach our dead-line.

In proof of what I have written about our 'terrible climate' I may mention that my grandfather worked in the Colony from 1844 to 1883, my father from 1879 to 1917, and I since 1905. It would be great fun to knock up the century, as cricketers say, but that hardly seems possible. Anyway, whatever the future holds, my family has nothing but thanks to Singapore; it has provided us all with a good living, most of which we have spent where we earned it, and in it we have been happy and healthy. That a white family can sojourn in Singapore for three generations without mental or physical deterioration is, I think, proved by the fact that my second brother, Darcy, is one of London's leading domestic architects; my youngest brother, Maurice, is the author of a play which has just closed a London run of more than 260 performances;[1] and my cousin, R. L. L. Braddell, was an Oxford double Blue and inter-

[1] *It's You I Want*, produced at Daly's Theatre by Mr. Seymour Hicks.

national footballer. Looking back, we can at least be proud that when we go out we shall go as purely white as when we came in, and weakened in no other way.

An ambitious man would hoot with laughter at the idea of spending his professional life in a place like Singapore, and doubtless the only outlet for ambition which it presents is a very slender chance of achieving a piece of coloured ribbon with an enamel appendage, or a title to be shared with so many others and for such varying reasons that discrimination between the merits of its holders is almost impossible. My grandfather received the former for his services as Attorney-General of the Colony, and my father the latter, since he held the position now called Chief Justice of the Federated Malay States; but neither of them was an ambitious man, they just did their jobs as they saw them.

In any event ambition is a will-o'-the-wisp, and to me it appears that the really important thing is to find work that interests one, to do it to the best of one's ability, and to make the most of this life, whether there is another or not; and I assert that a man can live an even fuller life, both professionally and otherwise, in Singapore than he can in England. Here he will have a greater multiplicity of interests and a much wider field of work, since he cannot specialize; here he will rub shoulders with a much greater diversity of fellow-men and become conversant with a much wider range of human customs and beliefs; here, too, he will have a much better chance of seeing the world at large, west and east. Finally, it is better to shoot at a clay pipe and hit a clay pipe than shoot at a star and break a ground-floor window.

Anyway, that's my story and I stick to it; so let's put out the lights and go to bed.